H.R.LOYN

The Making of the English Nation

From the Anglo-Saxons to Edward I

With 54 illustrations

THAMES AND HUDSON

For Pat

CONTENTS

PREFACE

The title of this book is a shade provocative. There was a time when the word 'nation' was sacrosanct, inadmissible without a multitude of qualifying adjectives. No nation could be recognized as such unless it had the full apparatus of a modern nation and state to support it. Such fineness and delicacy of definition led to an enfeeblement of vocabulary and, ultimately, to a distortion of thought. Modern lexicographers, mindful of past dispute, revert to a more generalized sense of the word. The *Concise Oxford English Dictionary* attempts 'congeries of people, either of diverse races or of common descent, language, history etc., inhabiting a territory bounded by defined limits'. Within this general framework there can be no doubt of the nationhood of England by 1300; indeed, the England of Edgar, Cnut and William I slides easily under the definition. Where lexicographers lead, historians should follow. It is certainly no anachronism to talk of the English nation in the reign of Edward I.

The situation within Britain is most clear-cut in England, though similar developments were also taking place in other communities within the British Isles, developments that were to lead to the idea and, with varying degrees of success, the reality of nationhood among the Scottish, the Welsh and the Irish. We shall not be primarily concerned with these developments, except where they play a vital part in the English story; our terms of reference confine us essentially to England. The chronological range extends from the fifth and sixth centuries, with the first formulation of recognizable political units by the Anglo-Saxon peoples in Britain, to the reign of the powerful Edward I, conqueror of Wales, under whose direction England seemed at one time well set to achieve permanent political mastery over the whole of the British Isles. The central thread of analysis is inevitably political, but full attempt is made to treat the important economic and social attributes of English history. Throughout nearly all of the period the church had a vital role to play in all aspects of life, and, indeed, most of our information about historical events and ideas has been transmitted through ecclesiastical sources. We have therefore given proper measure to religious history, both in its institutional ecclesiastical aspects and in its more abstract, philosophic attributes.

Evidence drawn from architectural and archaeological sources has been exceptionally useful in filling out the bare bones of the purely literary record. We have tried throughout to keep the European context in mind; parallels and occasional contrasts with the situation in other parts of Western Europe are at times striking, reminding us that similar economic motifs were present on the Continent, welding peoples of similar stock to the inhabitants of Britain into their historic shapes. Even so, generalized similarities are only part of the story. Peculiar virtues and vices are the stuff of historical analysis, and it is hoped that something of the special nature of English insular development will be brought out in the following pages.

Acknowledgments

In a book with no footnotes it is all the more necessary to thank my fellow historians, some of whose work is mentioned in the bibliography, for all they have done to clarify the picture of the growth of the English nation. My special thanks go to my friends and former colleagues, Dr Clive Knowles, Dr David Bates and Miss Brenda Bolton, who have read the proofs and saved me from several errors and infelicities. For those that remain I am of course solely responsible. I wish also to thank the staff at Thames and Hudson for the courteous and helpful way they have guided a complicated text through the press.

CHAPTER 1

The historical geography of England

Bede, the greatest historian to flourish in the early Middle Ages, started his ecclesiastical history of the English people with a full geographical description of Britain. Most of the physical details came from earlier writers: Pliny, Gildas, Solinus and Orosius. Britain was said to be 800 miles in extent from north to south, 200 miles in breadth (except where several promontories stretch further), and the whole circuit of the coastline, 4875 miles. When it came to discussing its natural wealth, Bede drew more on his personal knowledge. Britain was rich in crops and trees and had good pasture for cattle and beasts of burden. Vines could be grown in some districts, and there was plenty of land- and waterfowl. The rivers abounded in fish, especially salmon and eels; there were seals, dolphins, even whales. Shellfish were to be found: mussels (with pearls of every colour) and whelks from which a beautiful red dye could be produced. Salt springs, hot springs, metals of all sorts, also some jet, added to Bede's picture of a land flowing with milk and honey. Written as it was in early eighth-century Northumbria, that picture provides eloquent and accurate testimony to one of the basic facts of English history. The whole island of Britain, and especially the eastern and southern lowlands, was a fertile land. Given freedom from war, pestilence and plague, human communities could flourish and multiply within its boundaries.

Classical authors and personal information were enough to provide Bede with a sure basis to his geography. He also applied the same techniques, which he saw as part of the 'true law of history', to the much more difficult task of describing the origins of the peoples of England. In a famous passage he set out what was clearly current thought concerning English ancestry:

They came from three very powerful Germanic tribes, the Saxons, Angles and Jutes. The people of Kent and the inhabitants of the Isle of Wight are of Jutish origin and also those opposite the Isle of Wight, that part of the kingdom of Wessex which is still today called the nation of the Jutes. From the Saxon country, that is the district now known as Old Saxony, came the East Saxons and South Saxons and the West Saxons. Besides this, from the country of the Angles, that is the land between the kingdoms of the Jutes and the Saxons which is called *Angulus*, came the East Angles, the Middle Angles, the Mercians, and all the Northumbrian race (that is those people who dwell north of the river Humber) as well as the other Anglian peoples. *Angulus* is said to have remained deserted from that day to this.

The inadequacies and limitations of this passage have been much discussed in the last generation, notably by those eager to confirm a substantial degree of continuity from Roman Britain to Anglo-Saxon England and by those anxious to ensure that the ethnic Germanic elements did not overshadow the ethnic Celtic contributions to the making of the island communities. Even so, the passage remains fundamental to our understanding and gives at the very least a firm and intelligent basis for the discussion of English political life in Britain.

The communities Bede described – those living in Kent, Essex, Sussex, Wessex, East Anglia, Middle Anglia, Mercia and Northumbria – formed the raw material out of which an English church had been created and from which, ultimately, was to emerge a single kingdom of England. At the time he wrote there were at least seven kingdoms, the so-called Heptarchy (and Middle Anglia), their physical nature fitting in well with the notion of migration from Germanic lands and a river-valley penetration through the three principal points of entry from the east: the Thames, the Wash and the Humber/Trent system. Bede provided in clear Latin prose the agreed picture of origins common to the ruling groups in the Heptarchy. They thought of themselves as Germanic; they recognized their ancestors as migrants who had settled in substantial numbers, sufficient to leave deserted territory behind them in

Denmark. Where the detail can be tested, as in the reference to distinctive settlers opposite the Isle of Wight (the Meonware) or to the special importance of *Angulus* (Angeln in Denmark), it stands as plausible. Elsewhere in Europe other good writers in these centuries, though none as keen and precise as Bede, attempted similar literary tasks, establishing legitimate origins for Germanic rulers of subject Romanic peoples. Gregory of Tours (d. 594) had already done so for the Franks and Isidore of Seville (d. 636) for the Visigoths. Paul the Deacon (d. 799) was to perform a similar task for the Lombards during the later years of the reign of Charlemagne (768–814). Creation of such proto-national myths is perilous country even within the writer's own conventions. Other literary evidence may be scarce, but it is by no means non-existent and can cast shadows on the apparent certainties.

Even more important is the evidence drawn from the archaeological and linguistic record. Bede made no mention of the Frisians, and yet their distinctive pottery constitutes an important part of the archaeological record for the migration to England. There is a distinct possibility that migrants from south Sweden and Norway may have contributed significant elements in the making of East Anglia. The political divisions of the eighth century were the base units in Bede's own political thought and the channels through which he collected his information. He was naturally inclined to assume too readily that their specific identity could be carried back further than was justifiable. Even so, the fact that he could present a logical case on origins, based on existing political divisions, is an important pointer to eighth-century attitudes, as well as to the nature of the fifth- and sixth-century movements, the 'folk-wandering' of the Germanic peoples.

For no matter how much we might now reject the notion of pure racial or ethnic movements, there can be no doubt but that the creation of England was a product of that folk movement in northwest Europe. Angles, Saxons, Jutes and Frisians, a collection of predominantly West German people drawn in substantial numbers from the North Sea littoral, stretching from the Cymbric peninsula to the Frisian Isles, undertook that most difficult of operations, a migration by sea, and set up permanent homes within the boundaries of the Roman Empire in Roman Britain. The contrast with Germanic movements elsewhere in Western Europe was profound, and no discussion of the making of England can fail to take such a contrast into account. Yet we must constantly remind ourselves that the Germanic elements, important though they were, constituted part, and part only, of the fabric of early Britain.

It is as well first to touch on these points of contrast before turning to the highly complex and contentious problems connected with the chronology and nature of the English settlement in Britain. First and foremost there is the language question. In no other part of the western Roman Empire was the contrast between the early fifth and the early seventh century so complete. Ruling groups among the Franks, the Goths, the Burgundians or the Vandals might continue to use their native German speech in their military and aristocratic circles, but the bulk, the overwhelming majority, of their subjected peoples spoke Latin in recognizable form, and Latin dominated to form the base for medieval French, Occitan, Spanish and Italian. In Britain, alone among the substantial parts of the western Empire, there was a complete language change. The organized Celtic communities, it is true, retained their Celtic speech with significant Latin influence upon it. But in England the common language that we call Anglo-Saxon or Old English persisted as the dominant tongue, completely Germanic in structure, syntax and vocabulary, initially with negligible influence from Latin and with no significant influence whatsoever from the Celtic side. This is a social fact of the first importance in any assessment of the Anglo-Saxon invasions, and one that demands explanation. Coupled with this language phenomenon is the allied question of place-name structure. We must turn to this again in our discussion of chronology. The richness, complexity and variation from region to region in the English scene provide possible clues both to the nature and the timing of fifth- and sixth-century settlement. For the moment, while not denying parallels as well as contrasts, notably in the north and east of France, one can point to a special intensity of Germanic settlement names in some parts of England that is hard to parallel elsewhere in the western Empire.

And then there is the question of religion. The Empire of which

Roman Britain had been an integral part was a Christian empire. Bishops, priests and deacons existed; theologians flourished – one at least, Pelagius, to the point where his teachings were regarded by no less a figure than the great St Augustine of Hippo himself (d. 430) as dangerous heresy; martyrs were honoured, and it seems likely that special veneration was already paid to St Alban at Verulamium. The Celtic peoples in Wales, Cornwall and elsewhere in the western parts of what was to become historic England preserved their faith and intensified it under the heavy political and social pressures of the age, setting up great schools, such as that at Llantwit Major, and proselytizing their fellow Celts in Ireland and in the north among the Picts and Scots. They even cultivated their own special brand of Latin – Hisperic, artificial, abounding in extravagant borrowings of obscure words from the Greek – as if to emphasize their cultural affinities with the civilized world of the Mediterranean at a time when physical contact was precarious and dangerous. The contrast with the Anglo-Saxons could scarcely be more bleak. These Germanic peoples of whom Bede spoke were pagan and polytheistic, worshipping the gods of the German pantheon – Woden, Thor, Tiw, Freya – and tracing the ancestry of their rulers back to Woden himself. England again was unique. Elsewhere, the Germanic invaders were either Christian before they set out on their wandering or were quickly converted. It is true that most of the groups reckoned as East Germans – Visigoths, Ostrogoths, Vandals – held to a belief based on the teaching of the priest Arius, which was regarded as heretical by the orthodox Trinitarian populations among whom they settled; but Christian they were, even to the point of possessing the scriptures in their own tongue. Among the West Germans, the Franks under Clovis (480–511) affected a seasonable conversion to orthodox Trinitarian belief with no intermediary stage of Arianism, and part of their conspicuous political success has been attributed to the consequent identity of interest forged between Frankish rulers and subject peoples who were also co-religionists. East of the Rhine the Germans continued in their pagan ways, notably among the Old Saxons and the Frisians, but whenever they settled within the *limites* of Rome, they accepted Christianity – except in England. For more than a century (indeed, in many respects for nearer two centuries) a pagan wedge was inserted into what had been the uniform Christian world of the western Empire – again, a matter that demands explanation.

Peculiarities in language, place-names and religion appear also to be mirrored in substantial institutional changes that provide a contrast with most of the Continent. There is, to begin with, the question of towns. The names survived – London, York, Exeter, a multiplicity of 'chesters' – but such survival is primarily interpreted as the survival of names as landmarks or at best habitation sites, certainly not as urban institutions in any meaningful sense of the term. Gildas, writing his religious polemics in the mid-sixth century, does not rank among the most convincing and authoritative of writers, but when he lamented that all the twenty-eight cities of Roman Britain had fallen into decay, he expressed what was surely his contemporary view of the urban situation. Anglo-Saxon super-stitious dread of deserted Roman towns, the old work of giants, represents one side of the picture, though historians and archaeo-logists have been at one in tracing and extolling the revival of urban life and institutions, culminating in what is seen virtually as a burghal policy under Alfred and his successors.

Nevertheless, little evidence has been found of urban life in Britain between the early fifth century and the seventh. In Canter-bury, where expectations were high of some sort of continuity, presumably associated with contact with Frankia, excavations have been disappointing, revealing layers of black soil that mark a dramatic break between Roman and Anglo-Saxon occupation. Simi-lar layers elsewhere at many Roman sites, Gloucester, Leicester, London, Cirencester, Chichester, Winchester and York, have been subject to great variation in interpretation. Some appear, indeed, to indicate a certain decisive break between two ages; at others, the possibility exists that the soil may represent an alteration of use, even agricultural use, within the farmed urban areas. Some towns were already in steep decline in the fourth century. Even at Verulamium (St Albans), where there is strong evidence for conti-nued occupation into the fifth century, it is clear that the theatre was already used as a rubbish dump for the nearby market before 400. London was referred to as a metropolis in the seventh century, but

13

archaeological evidence for continuation of urban life through the fifth century remains elusive in the extreme, and modern attention has been focused on the growth of Aldwych further up the Thames as much as on the Roman city itself. At Winchester, where intense and probing archaeology has had vigorous civic support, virtually no finds have been made that can be credited to the period between *c.* 450 and 650.

General urban decline in the West and the possible presence of German mercenaries in some late fourth-century British towns muddy the picture, but again the cumulative evidence points to peculiar development that demands discussion. In Frankia towns survived as significant habitation sites, often prominent as centres from which Christian bishops operated. England appears to have been quite different and more dramatically non-urban. It is possible here that there was some contrast also with the indigenous Romano-Britons of the west, who preserved some vestige of urban existence late. This depends on the weight we put on the evidence of the Anglo-Saxon Chronicle, which marks a decisive move in the process (as it sees it) of Anglo-Saxon conquest with the capture of Glouces-ter, Cirencester and Bath in 577, and on evidence that Chester retained special importance as late as the second decade of the seventh century. But archaeologists, assessing work already done at Gloucester, Cirencester, Worcester, Chester and Carlisle, note some survival into the fifth century, some evidence for timber building, here and there of substantial size, but nothing to disturb the general picture of a decisive break between late Roman occupation (when urban economy was already in a bad way) and later use of site. The English were not town-dwellers, and towns elsewhere in Britain suffered decay and decline in the course of the fifth and sixth centuries. Only towards the last quarter of the sixth century is there hint of some revival in the south-east, as contacts firmed up between Canterbury and London and the Frankish kingdoms.

On the surface, equal dramatic contrast between Britain and the Continent occurred in relation to rural institutions. The best known among these institutions was, of course, the villa. Attempts at close definition of the term have led to as much dispute as, for example, over definitions of the medieval manor, but some points are clear. In late Roman days the term was used of a dwelling in the country, normally the centre of an agrarian enterprise, though sometimes with important industrial attributes, notably those connected with textiles. At their most luxurious, with mosaics, baths and the general feel of civilized living, villas represented rich elements of Romanization, providing echoes of life in the fourth-century Cotswolds that sound back to the ideal rural scenes of Horace, Virgil or Pliny. A villa could also be little more than an upgraded native farm. The villa system, if such it can be called, suffered from invasion and peasant unrest in late Roman Gaul, though Britain, surprisingly, has yielded traces of a definite increase in villa prosperity in the fourth century, possibly stimulated by some movement of prosperous landowners from Gaul to its comparative safety at that stage. However this may be – and the possibility of a shift among the prosperous classes away from the towns must also be taken into account – villas throughout the Western world depended as institutions on the apparatus of an imperial economy with a relatively wide-ranging market, and these conditions ceased to exist in the fifth century.

Even so, contrasts abound. In France and Belgium the practice of using villa buildings as places of burial was extremely common. In Britain known examples are rare, though widespread: Llantwit Major (Glamorgan), Banwell (Somerset), Denton and Worlaby (Lincs.), Great Tew and Wiggington (Oxon.), Southwell Minster (Notts.), Well House (Berks.). Evidence for continued use as religious buildings, connected with monasteries or directly converted to church use, is significant in Gaul and virtually non-existent in Britain. The admittedly treacherous field of place-name study provides further food for thought. Literally hundreds of villa names have survived, notably in north France and Belgium, carrying names of late Roman or early medieval estate-owners, usually with the suffix '-acus' or '-acum', through to the modern world. We have yet to recognize a single surviving name in Britain.

Allowance has to be made for intense regional variation and for topographical variation within regions, but the overall trend of modern thought is to stress continuity in Gaul, though through twisted paths, from late Roman villa to medieval manor. The buildings did not survive, but the fields did. Concentration on the villa as a house is understandable; the Romans built in stone and brick, tiles and mosaics, so leaving visual evidence to posterity. Such evidence may be heavily misleading, however. Side by side with Roman or Romanized villas there continued to exist Celtic farms, hamlets, villages, and it is more than likely that under the pressure of barbarian settlement and the creation of new Germanic king-doms, the medieval village, with attendant dominical manor houses, was freshly created. As John Percival, our leading interpreter of the agrarian scene in these centuries, has put it succinctly: 'the dere-liction of farm land was by no means as extensive as the villa ruins might otherwise have suggested'. Food had to be grown, and no one willingly clears land if old clearings are still available. An amalgam of villa fields and Romano-Gaulish Celtic communities under new leadership, living close to the soil and in timber halls, could bring out the new agrarian base for Merovingian and Carolingian civilization. The peasant was indeed now firmly fixed on his plot.

But was Britain so different from Gaul? Do we put too much weight on the linguistic and religious differences? With so much uncertainty, it would be rash to attempt anything other than an interim judgment. The Germanic newcomers in the fifth and sixth centuries had special skills at forest-clearing and at growing cereal crops in the variable climate of north-west Europe, which they presumably exploited to the full in the favourable conditions of the east and south of Britain. Even allowing for the existence of the heavy plough in Roman days and for more intense valley settlement than was thought likely a generation ago, the Anglo-Saxons appear at the very least to have intensified a valley-ward drift, favouring their islands of gravel in valleys of clay. Regional variation is dramatic. In the south-east many Romano-British sites were aban-doned. In the north and west there was certainly greater continuity in population, but there is also evidence for change, a tendency to re-use old hill forts such as Cadbury (Congresbury), Cadbury Castle (where a break between Roman and post-Roman occupation seems certain), and Maiden Castle in Dorset. Much constructive work has been done on the Upper Thames valley, and the upshot of archaeo-logical investigation there suggests a contraction of settlements in later Roman days, followed by intensification under new Germanic direction throughout the fifth century.

In the last resort our interpretation depends on our picture of the German migrant and our assessment of numbers relative to the surviving British population. Our interpretation of this period of change is complex, and so was the reality. In 400 we confront evidence for rural life in an empire in decline: villas, hamlets, agglomerations of dwellings attached to decaying towns and villas, and even something akin to our later villages. In 600 we suspect a vastly different picture over much of the country we now begin to call England: a significant presence of consolidated villages, and yet survivals of Roman and Celtic communities in enclaves, and also in conjunction with, and integrated with, the Anglo-Saxon newcomers. Ethnic integrity is not to be expected, even if ethnic myths flourish, and the *wealhas*, or Welsh, or slaves, are distinguished from the English settlers. The period of change was violent, and the language of contemporaries who attempted to describe it, apocalyptic. Yet fire and the sword, rape and pillage, did not universally dominate the story. By the end of the sixth century a degree of stability had been achieved which meant the provision of food and shelter, and protection sufficient to enable human communities to survive and flourish. The hierarchic, Germanic-speaking communities of early England made a radical legal division in their societies between the free and the unfree. It is likely that Romano-British survivors constituted a significant element among the unfree, possibly in some districts exercising traditional crafts as shepherds, cattle-raisers, bee-keepers and the like. But slaves cannot be kept in their unfree place unless the dominant group is truly dominant, in full military, physical, and consequent legal and social control. This simple fact, coupled with the linguistic and religious evidence, is enough to suggest that the migration of the dominant, free, Germanic-speaking groups from their Continental homes was large-scale. In a colonizing situation and an agrarian economy, a thin veneer of Anglo-Saxon landlords would not have been able to bring about the changes we know occurred in Britain. Indeed, they would have been lucky to survive.

There are two general features of the archaeological record that enable us to gauge the extent of these changes: the evidence drawn from our knowledge of the pottery and the coinage. They are interconnected. Manufacture of pottery for a substantial market virtually demanded the existence of a society where money formed a principal means of exchange, and it is no surprise therefore to find that both ceased to be a feature of British society from the early fifth century. Already in the late fourth century there is evidence of decline in the quality of Romano-British pottery, in its range of decoration and form of vessel, but of the major kiln groups most were still in operation up to 400, producing types identifiable as Alice Holt, Dorset black-burnished, Hadham, Nene Valley, New Forest and Oxfordshire. The removal of Roman forces in the first decade of the fifth century probably provided the final blow to an industry already in decline. Individual potters of course remained, some working for new Germanic masters, but the old system of mass production, primarily for military and urban markets, ceased. Careful discussion of the nature of the so-called Romano-Saxon type of pottery is leading to the rejection of the view that significant Germanic settlement took place in fourth-century Roman Britain, though it is freely accepted that in Britain, as on the Continent, barbarian adaptation of Roman artifacts was commonly practised. But certainly by the middle of the fifth century, and probably for a whole generation before that arbitrary date, manufacture on any wide scale was a thing of the past, and the making of pottery a matter for local craftsmen operating in a cramped, localized agrarian setting.

Coinage presents a much more dramatic picture and, unless completely unexpected and unforeseen archaeological finds turn up to confound us, gives factual evidence of change that must be carefully considered. Up to the opening years of the fifth century Britain remained an integral part of an empire, much of whose economic activity depended on the free flow of money, authorized, struck and supervised by imperial officers. Gold, silver and bronze coins were relatively abundant in the south and the east up to about 400, but then tail off rapidly with few dated after 404, though some more silver coins of Honorius, struck c. 420, have been found near Chelmsford in Essex and in Coleraine, Co. Londonderry. There is no evidence at all that any coinage was struck in Britain until the seventh century. The general implications of such a phenomenon are clear. The need for coined money disappeared with the apparatus of imperial government, the civil service, the army that had to be paid, the fiscal system that kept the administrative and military machine alive. This is not true of most of Gaul, Spain, Italy and North Africa, where tax systems, methods of administering estates, land measurements and coinage persisted, if barbarized. The loss of coinage, the absence of Christianity in English England, and the language changes that left a Celtic vernacular dominant in the west with a Germanic in the east constitute the main points in argument for those who wish to emphasize the catastrophic effects of the turmoil of the fifth and sixth centuries in Britain, as opposed to all other areas of the western Empire where Romanism visibly survived.

The changes that came over Britain in these centuries were indeed in many respects greater than those that occurred elsewhere in the western Empire. Numerous general reasons for this can be given, all of which probably represent some facet of the truth. It could be that Britain, being further from the Mediterranean fulcrum, was less Romanized than Gaul, always retaining some of the attributes of a frontier province. It could be that the Germanic invaders were particularly backward, pagan, and only hesitantly touched by Rome. It could be – a view that I favour myself – that the movement was more specifically agrarian than elsewhere, launched by men and women who were true migrants, seeking new land to settle. One feature of the initial stages of the Anglo-Saxon settlement is unquestioned and vital for understanding. It was thorough, but long-drawn-out. Dramatic events connected with the withdrawal of troops from Roman Britain took place in the first decade of the fifth century; dramatic events at Rome, which resulted in the launching of the move to bring back England to the Roman Christian fold, took place in the last decade of the sixth century. Close on two centuries lay between these two known and well-authenticated points, and precious little historical evidence has survived to tell us directly what happened in between. Similar puzzles faced the good historians of the age when they tried to reconstitute events, and it might be well now to look back to Bede to see how he treated the chronology and the nature of the Anglo-Saxon settlement, the beginning of England.

There are some features of Bede's account that infuriate the modern reader. His proper purpose was to write ecclesiastical history, and we would willingly sacrifice his long account of the martyrdom of St Alban, his short note on the martyrs Aaron and Julian, his comment on the Arian heresy of Pelagius, and the detail on the visits of St Germanus to Britain to combat heresy, in return for more hard fact on the Anglo-Saxons. Even so, within his limits and purpose he gives a logical picture. His context is the fall of the Empire in the West, and he says so. With Valentinian (d. 455) the western Empire fell (*cum quo simul Hesperium concidit regnum*). In Britain he attributed the disaster to the withdrawal of troops to sustain the bids of tyrants for political ends (Maximus, the *municeps* Gratian, Constantine), the failure of the British to maintain their own defence, and the ferocity of attacks from outside, from the Irish and the Picts. He acknowledged the good will of the Romans even after they ceased to rule in Britain, an event he associated directly with the capture of Rome by the Goths in 410, the 1164th year after its foundation and almost 470 years after Gaius Julius Caesar had come to these islands. Twice they sent 'legions' to support the provincials, and Bede wove his own false interpretation of the building of the northern walls into his story of Roman success. After the second intervention they told the Britons they could no longer afford such ventures, and there followed an apocalyptic period. The Irish and the Picts indulged in massacre and looting. The Britons increased their external calamities by internal strife, 'until the whole land was left without food and destitute except for such relief as hunting brought'. There followed the unsuccessful appeal to the consul Aetius (d. 454), who was unable to help them because of the devastation caused by Attila, by famine and by plague. Britain also suffered but rallied, initiated a period of recovery, prosperity, positive luxury with all its attendant evils – enough to prompt its king Vortigern to take the fatal step of inviting the Saxons to help against the Picts and the Irish. The Saxons arrived in their three warships, were granted a place of settlement in the east, won a great victory and were joined by a massive band of warriors from their homeland, which made them an invincible army. They then turned against their paymasters allying with the Picts, until Ambrosius Aurelianus, the last of the Romans, rallied the Britons.

Drawing his material from Gildas, Bede makes the next decisive point in the story the siege of Mount Badon, some forty-four years after the Saxon arrival in Britain, at which the Britons slaughtered no small number of their foes. One can sense how Bede, struggling to make sense out of Gildas's knowledge of imperial and ecclesiastical history, reached his conclusions about two critical events: the advent of the Saxons and their settlement in the east about 450, and the setback to their advance through a decisive rally of the British that prevented complete conquest some forty-four years later. His apparent precision on Mount Badon came from a misunderstanding of Gildas, but even so the theme of British revival may well be based on fact. Literary evidence suggests, perhaps in simplistic terms, that the Saxons, successful in settlement and bent on conquest, reached a halting-place in their advance give or take a decade or so of 500. Bede completes his narrative with a long flashback to the visits of St Germanus to Britain in the first half of the fifth century and a further short chapter (his only comment on much of the sixth century) that again draws on Gildas to talk of a time when Britain was free from external, though not from internal, wars – a time when the Roman virtues (as Bede saw them) of truth and justice were lost. As a proem to the conversion of the English, Bede makes the special charge that the Britons never preached the faith to the Saxons and the Angles, but of the internal history of the Anglo-Saxons he says not a word.

Surprisingly little is added to this basic picture by the Anglo-Saxon Chronicle. The compilers, working at the court of King Alfred, knew their Bede and set their chronological guidelines at the fall of Rome in 410, the appeal to Aetius in the 440s, and the invitation to the Saxons in the imperial reign of Mauritius (Martianus) and Valentinian (448–55). They then wove into their narrative, in scrappy and repetitive form, simple statements abstracted from genealogies and oral poetry, which add some details that have become part of the national myth but which do little to tell us what truly happened: the identification of the land settled by Hengest and Horsa as the south-east rather than the east, as in Bede; Hengest's genealogy taken back to Woden; a succession of battles, associated with place-names and invoking heroic leader-figures: Aelle of the South Saxons, Cerdic and his son Cynric of the West Saxons, Ida of the Northumbrians, Cuthwulf, who, as late as 571, is said to have fought against the Britons and to have captured four towns (all with good Saxon elements to their names) at Limbury, Aylesbury, Bensington and Eynsham, and Cuthwine and Ceawin, who captured Gloucester, Cirencester and Bath in 577 after defeating and killing three British kings at the battle of Dyrham. There is no mention of Mount Badon. All the political entries refer to Saxon victories. Selective memory (or imagination) has clearly been at work. Elegy of the type found in the great Old Welsh praise-poem, the *Gododdin*, is conspicuously lacking. A set of laudatory verses set side by side with pagan genealogies and fitted in somewhat haphazardly to fifth- and sixth-century chronology is the most likely source for this section of the Chronicle.

And yet for all the disappointment of the jejune nature of the entries, the Chronicle helps to confirm one special point that is essential for any discussion of the origins of England: quite simply, that the process of Anglo-Saxon conquest and settlement was slow, long-drawn-out, extending over at least four, if not five, generations even before St Augustine and his missionaries arrived in Kent. Shrewd observers also note that the same type of entry tends to be interwoven with good solid material from Bede in the Chronicle's account of the seventh century. The effective occupation of historic England up to the bounds of Cornwall, Wales, and an indeterminate line with the Cumbrians and the Picts, overlapped with the process of conversion and could not be said to be anything like complete until the mid-seventh century and the Synod of Whitby (663). Celtic sources confirm the general picture. Gildas, in the middle of the sixth century, wrote in a land of settled part-Roman Celtic tribal kingship, still very conscious of its Romanism and Christianity. The Lives of the Saints – Illtyd, Samson, David, to mention only three of the more influential – take for granted a Christian ascetic background that embraced the Brythonic world of Wales, Cornwall and Brittany and was biting deep into the Goidelic communities of

Ireland and Scotland. Political legends of Maximus, of Emrys Wledig (Ambrosius) and ultimately, through poetry and romance, of Arthur point in the same direction. The creation of political England was no walk-over. Bede's instinctive recreation of the chronology from the unsatisfactory mishmash of evidence may well have been near the truth: two generations of concentrated settlement in the east (c.450–500), two generations of uneasy stability (500–50), two generations and more of decisive Anglo-Saxon political advance (c.550–650). And it would be essentially during the period of stability that the historic tribal kingdoms took initial shape among both the Anglo-Saxon and surviving British communities.

A chronological pattern of this type could certainly fit with one important source of evidence still capable of yielding precious insight: that is, the evidence of place-names. The complexities here are immense: lack of early written forms, hesitations over transmission from one language to another, uncertainty over sequence of type and meaning. Some names, such as those of large rivers, like the Thames, mountain ranges or great towns, are likely to survive even massive dislocations of human society and population. Kent and Lincoln stand out as two great territorial names transmitted directly from Roman days. Some British names, such as Dover and Wendover, preserve their identity even in inflected forms – *dofras*, the waters, is a plural – into the Anglo-Saxon language. Place-name evidence for final settlement does not always help as one tries to grapple with the chronology of settlement, though the absolute contrast of, for example, the overwhelmingly Celtic nature of place-names in Cornwall and the equally overwhelming Germanic nature of habitation names in Surrey, Sussex or the East Riding of Yorkshire (taking later Scandinavian into account) tells us much in crude terms of settlement patterns.

Most revealing from the point of view of our immediate problem is evidence taken from the naming of small rivers and streams. These, more than any other type are likely to reveal the dominant speech patterns of agrarian settlers dependent on them for their water supply. Close examination of these names suggests a three-fold division in historic England that could fit in well to the three stages in Anglo-Saxon settlement postulated above. The first area consists roughly of England east of a line drawn from the Yorkshire Wolds to the east of Salisbury Plain, and so to the Hampshire coast near Southampton – essentially the river valleys draining from the highland spine of England to the sea between Flamborough Head and the Solent. Celtic names are limited in number and nature, and the area, with its heavy Germanic content of small river names, would correspond well to a region of primary agrarian settlement in depth by Germanic-speaking peoples. The second area consists of the highland spine itself from the Pennines and the Cotswolds, to Salisbury Plain and the valley of the Hampshire Avon. Within this compass British words are more numerous, and the area would correspond happily with territory absorbed by the rising kingdoms of Wessex, Mercia and Northumbria in the period *c*.550–650. The third area consists of rivers draining west, the Lake District, most of Lancashire, the Welsh Marches and the south-west to the Tamar. Here British waterways are common and there are more surviving British habitation names. This is also the area where we find most of the major Saxon 'settler' names, the *Wreocensætan* in Shropshire, the *Magonsætan* in Herefordshire, the *Sumorsætan* in Somersetshire. If a substantial British enclave survived in the Chilterns, the presence of the form *Cilternsætan*, helps gently to substantiate the picture of a final stage in the consolidation of English England as late as the later seventh century.

A plausible picture therefore exists for the chronology of the Anglo-Saxon settlement, and a slow, tortuous progress it turns out to be. Grave doubts still persist on the nature of these settlements. Stories of extermination, famine, plague and pestilence are too strong to be ignored but are countered by stories of revival, prosperity, glimpses of a brief Golden Age. Evidence of fire and devastation, and ominous layers of black earth are countered by evidence of imported fine ware at Cadbury Castle, Cadbury (Congresbury), Tintagel and Dinas Powys. The exquisite craftsmanship of the Kentish jewelry of the pagan period in the later seventh century hints at a degree of opulence that should not be ignored. Better knowledge of Third World conditions have taught us that human societies with a relatively low subsistence base can recover rapidly from the most appalling disasters, whether natural or caused by human folly and wickedness, and that the ruling groups can quickly acquire great wealth. Saviours from disaster can name their own price. Even so, it would be rash not to recognize the fifth and sixth centuries as one of the truly regressive periods in British history. Roman Britain, even in its declining years, was still part of a civilized, Mediterranean-based empire. It had a literate and Christian element in its population, was accustomed to the use of coinage, and still enjoyed to some degree the advantages of inter-regional trade of a territorial empire. The English kingdoms which St Augustine and his companions approached with understandable caution, were pagan, illiterate and German-speaking, not only at the top level but throughout society, as the missionaries and their successors later in the seventh century consistently recognized.

And yet the puzzle still remains. How much of Rome still survived? Among the Celtic populations the Christian religion, even if in a rather specialized form organizationally, carried much of Rome with it into the new and tribal kingdoms. Latin, methods of transmitting land by charter, notably in south-east Wales, even some awareness of imperial titles persisted. Among the Germans this was not obviously so, and yet better appreciation of the topography of settlement, even in areas of primary settlement such as Kent, the hundred of Dengie in Essex, or parts of south-east Suffolk, including the site of Sutton Hoo, has disclosed peculiarities that suggest elements of continuity in land divisions, boundaries and even possible field systems. The Anglo-Saxon moved in initially on terms. Their social organization laid special stress on the possession of a free kindred, and yet they were slave-owners. There is no evidence that they practised mass extermination after their initial brutal seizing of land and crops and possessions. One of the very few revealing passages of the Anglo-Saxon Chronicle, *sub anno* 491, registers a complete slaughter of the British inhabitants of Pevensey as something extraordinary, worthy of record. Yet my guess – and at this stage it can be little more – is that in the area of primary settlement where our Germanic river-names predominate there was relatively little significant Romano-British survival. The remarkable freedom of the Anglo-Saxon language from British influence, the overwhelming preponderance of Germanic habitation names in '-ham' and '-ton', in '-ingas', '-ingaham' and '-in-gaton', the certainty that the Saxons were themselves farmers not aristocrats divorced from the soil, the nature of their nucleated settlements and hamlets, their retention of paganism, build up a cumulative picture of a new order slowly and tenaciously held and developed in eastern England in the centuries 450–650.

It is hard to envisage Romano-British survival except in enclaves or as subordinate functional attributes to the dominant newcomers. The active elements in the Romano-Celtic population moved west, no difficult matter in Britain. As some cynical observers have commented, the Romans left two principal legacies to the British: their roads, to take them away from the new Germanic order of the east, and their religion, to console them in their hours of need. But this applies only to the area of initial settlement. As the German kingdoms stabilized and prospered, they extended their rule over the highland spine of England and beyond, and no one can deny a substantial ethnic element of British in the population there. In the later stages of expansion into Somerset and Devon, along the Welsh Marches and into Cumbria, a common religion held the population together. Anglo-Saxon law codes indicate significant elements of *Wealh* (Welsh) presence at quite high social levels in Wessex. By that stage the social and linguistic dominance of the Germanic-speaking population was such that the British conformed. Insular Latin was newly acquired by the converted Anglo-Saxons, often from Celtic teachers. But their vernacular, their institutions, even their kingship, emerged more stringently Germanic than those of any other people to settle within the Roman Empire.

There remains one final line of inquiry before moving into the relatively smooth waters of the conversion of the English to Christianity; and that concerns the question of the nature of their kingship. Fresh life has been given to this problem by the efforts of younger historians anxious to look beyond the generalizations of Bede to the nature of smaller units of settlement, the basic building blocks out of which the kingdoms were created. For the kingdoms were unquestionably made in England and made slowly in England. The clearest evidence comes from the Midland kingdom of Mercia, the latest of the larger units to achieve its historic shape. Mercia was the creation of the pagan Penda (626–54), accurately described by Wendy Davies as 'a great war leader who had made nonsense of the ethnic and religious divisions of his day'. When Penda was defeated and slain by King Oswy of Northumbria at the battle of Winwaed we hear of the thirty subordinate leaders who brought their forces to support him. Described as *duces regni* by Bede they represented a whole spectrum of relationship to the Mercian king, ranging from British kings and Ethelhere, the East Anglian king, to men who presumably had no higher status than that of provincial governor. Certainly, the Anglo-Saxon translator of Bede in the late ninth century found difficulty in describing their status, referring to them as *heretogan* and *ealdormen*, that is to say warleaders with a degree of independence, and also high-ranking but dependent officers. The Tribal Hidage, a document that sets out the tribute due from more than thirty dependent peoples and probably represents the fiscal ideal aimed at by a seventh-century Mercian king, gives a precious glimpse of the political groupings that underlay the smooth facade of the greater kingdoms. It is probable that many of these represent early groupings of Germanic settlers in pagan times, around Hitchin in Hertfordshire, for example, or Whittlesey Mere in Huntingdonshire. We know nothing of their terminology of leadership in those days, but it is not impossible that their leaders may have held a royal title. Certainly, if the Irish analogy is pressed, as many good scholars now wish, a host of petty independent kings is by no means an impossible model for sixth-century England, the leaders of successful colonists taking on the mantle of pagan lordship. Penda brought rationality and a degree of unification by his military prowess; his Christian successors completed the process and also, incidentally, helped to make the kingly title more special and exclusive.

Similar hints of the existence of coherent political units, Bede's *provinciæ* or *regiones*, can be found elsewhere. Kent, where the tradition of an initial agreement between Saxons and Britons is exceptionally strong, provides a special case. Delicate work, which involves sensitive handling of topography, historical geography and place-names, is helping to reconstruct knowledge of the primitive *regiones* of Kent. The four lathes of East Kent, with royal vills at Wye, Canterbury, Lympne and Eastry, seem to have existed from the early days of the kingdoms, whereas West Kent was divided initially into a single unit based on Rochester, and later into three unequal territories based on royal vills. Nicholas Brooks has suggested that these arrangements may point to a passing of West Kent under the rule of an East Kentish dynasty, an event that reached a decisive point in the reign of Ethelbert (d. 616), the king and overlord who first received Christianity into pagan England. Similar work is helping to uncover primitive sub-kingdoms elsewhere in England. Sussex bears a possible parallel to Kent. The earliest settlements were in the eastern half of the Sussex Downs, but by the sixth century all the downlands were under control, as King Aelle and his successors took command of the Roman *civitas* centred on Chichester. Common sense enters the story. Geographical and strategic facts that made for the choice of Roman or Romano-British administrative centres – river crossings, good harbours, position on roads – applied equally to those of the Anglo-Saxons. Based on assumptions over transhumance in economy and knowledge of early charters, possible patterns of administrative units can be constructed throughout the south-east. Our old certainty that names ending in '-ingas' or '-ingaham' indicated the earliest layer of settlement has proved to be unreliable, but modern investigation is bringing back the possibility that names such as Hastings, Woking, the Mallings, Godalming, the Basing of Basingstoke, Sonning and Reading may yet yield a clue to some at least of the smaller political units formed after the first generation of settlement, when political leadership began to assert itself on a permanent basis.

The situation among the Middle Saxons is infinitely complicated by our lack of knowledge of London, but there again attention is drawn to names that exist in the modern shires of Middlesex and adjoining Hertfordshire and Essex: Ealing (the home of the *Gillingas*), Harrow (the heathen temple, or *hearg*, of the *Gumeningas*), the Rodings in Essex, the *Mimmas* of North and South Mimms, the *Wæclingas* who inhabited Verulamium (St Albans), and a host of other possible names that may well reflect the moment when permanent shape was given to the new agrarian order by the recognized chieftain or head of family, the Gilla of Ealing or the Sunna of Sonning in Berkshire. There are hints everywhere of variation in settlement, and yet similarities in local consolidation of lordship over manageable areas. In East Anglia organization by early pioneers in the river valleys at the Lark, the Wavering and Sandlings was overtaken in historic times by a manorial system under royal control. In Northumbria the ancient names of the constituent kingdoms, Deira around York and Bernicia in the harder country further north, were preserved from Romano-Celtic times. In the Western Midlands we note a succession of names ending in *sætan* (or *sæte*) with their clear implications of related late colonizing names: the *Meresæte, Rhiwsæte, Halhsæte, Temesæte*, and *Stepelsæte* along the line later marked out by Offa's dyke.

Some of the shape of the fluid political groupings of these hidden centuries begins to emerge. But below those intermediate political divisions there still lurk great mysteries. Perhaps the most acute observations have been made in recent years by Thomas Charles Edwards, who, from his exact knowledge of the Celtic world, especially Ireland, was able to make observations on this fundamental problem of settlement. He reminded us of the limitations imposed in the fifth century on all colonizing ventures by the low range of mobility and lack of easy exchange of value implicit in coinage. Itineration became an essential economic base for these early kings, who had literally to travel on their circuits to eat up their renders, their bread, meat, drink and other provisions. In the larger kingdoms, as they developed, tribute took the place of food rent, tribute paid customarily in terms of livestock. If we apply these tests of reward for superiority to our early politics we gain a theoretical position that often proves close to reality, an inner core to the kingdom where the king can travel to receive his honourable *hospitalis* and an outer core from which tribute was expected. Great lords other than kings, *subreguli* or *prefecti*, would also enjoy similar renders and tribute. Bede's kings, the kings of the so-called Heptarchy, give us our historic foundation of the territorial kingdoms of England, but they themselves represent a critical stage in the creation of political power in the immigrant community, and a relatively late stage at that. Christianity and settled kingship then grew together, masking the infinite complexities of the small-scale political patterns of the fifth and sixth centuries.

CHAPTER 2

The conversion of the English to Christianity

There is a danger, since most of our knowledge of seventh-century England comes from the writings of Bede, that we underestimate consistently the novelty of the idea of Christian kingship. Bede was a great historian, but he was also a Christian monk, purposefully set on showing the need for accepting the new faith and critically aware of the benefits of its acceptance, even in material matters. Failure to appreciate the novelty has led to a resultant failure to appreciate the strength and originality of so many of the achievements of the early Middle Ages, not only in England but also throughout Continental Europe, where Franks, Visigoths, Suevi, Ostrogoths, Burgundians and Vandals carved out kingdoms for their Germanic peoples within the fabric of the Roman Empire in the West. It is true that the examples of Hebraic kingship and the Christian emperor Constantine could be potent when they settled among Christian peoples; the living example of Byzantium survived in the East. Yet the Germanic traditions of a different type of kingship were also strong, and nowhere stronger than in late sixth-century England. How, therefore, did it come about that the new Christian faith, with its deep social and consequent political implications, was received so readily and, as far as one can judge, completely in so short a time?

The course of the conversion is best read in terms of three generations of hard work, from the landing of St Augustine in Kent in 597 to the death of St Theodore of Tarsus, archbishop of Canterbury (668–90). Two groups of missionaries took part, identifiable and distinctive, though not as divergent as they were once considered, conveniently described as Roman and Celtic. The Roman missionaries came direct from Rome itself or from Frankia, the Celtic mostly from Ireland and their power centre at Iona, from which they spread to Lindisfarne and deep into the structure of virtually every English kingdom. British Christians from Cornwall, Wales and Cumbria do not appear to have played as prominent a part in the conversion as might be expected – indeed, quite the contrary – and written sources, notably Bede, are somewhat harsh about them in consequence. Bede's description of the Synod of Aust, where St Augustine failed to reach agreement with the British bishops, and his comments on the massacre of British monks at the hands of the pagans are symptoms of a consistent distrust of the British church. Modern scholarship is to some extent redressing the balance in suggesting a degree of quiet movement, especially in the north-west, in the Middle Kingdom and the western parts of Wessex.

In the first generation the initiative lay with the Romans. The inspiration behind the movement came from Pope Gregory himself (590–604); Bede tells the charming story of Gregory's concern at the sight of the English slave-boys in the market-place, beautiful of face but stained with their native paganism, and of his immediate resolve to bring them to the Christian faith by his own missionary efforts. This proved impossible, but after his succession to the papacy he sent Augustine with a powerful company of helpers and inter-preters to convert the English. Augustine turned back once, as he realized the daunting nature of the task, and it needed Gregory's exhortations and practical support, diplomatic as well as spiritual, to urge on the mission to the point where it landed, some forty strong, in the Isle of Thanet. King Ethelbert of Kent was then, in 597, the most powerful ruler in Britain. Though married to a Frankish princess who was herself a Christian, he was cautious in his reception of the mission, meeting them in the open air rather than an enclosed building for fear of witchcraft, and taking time and care to see what manner of men they were and what style of life they led before encouraging his people to accept the new faith. Once the court had been converted, the kingdom followed suit. Augustine continued to receive practical support and help from Rome, and he and his successors planted Christianity firmly at Canterbury, Rochester and London, and to some extent in Essex. Attempts by Paulinus further north to convert King Edwin of Northumbria achieved temporary success in 625–7, though Edwin's political defeat and death in 632 brought this phase of Roman missionary effort to a virtual end.

Bede, in telling the story of this phase in the conversion, does not minimize the hazards and tells of reversions to paganism and general hesitations and complications. Ethelbert's successor, Eadbald, and the successors to Saebert, king of Essex, turned back initially to the pagan faith. Redwald of East Anglia, the king and overlord most likely to be commemorated in the great ship-burial at Sutton Hoo, is said to have tried to get the best of both worlds, in having the Christian mysteries and pagan altars present in the same church. In two reflective passages Bede, in his typical parable-like style, gives penetrating insights into both the difficulties facing the missionaries and the reasons for their success. King Ethelbert is said to have hesitated long because he could not consent easily to accept the new promises and so to forsake the beliefs that he and the whole English race had held. An unnamed ealdorman at the court of King Edwin argued that the life of man was so fleeting (like the flight of a sparrow through a lighted hall, from winter into winter) that if the new doctrine brought more certain information, it should be accepted. Bede was right to emphasize the sophisticated religious strength of the new faith, rooted in Mediterranean belief and philosophy, but there were more practical reasons too that made Christianity the right religion for the times. It was a literate religion and carried with it civilized overtones in its attitudes to law, social discipline and Rome. One of Ethelbert's first reactions after the conversion was to issue a law code, according to the Roman example, which reconciled the new church to the social order of the kingdom. Intensified contact with the Continent and with Rome, which came in the train of the mission, enriched the life of the whole community.

The second generation of the conversion and the middle years of the century were dominated by the Celtic Christians. There were political reasons for this. An alliance of British Christians and the pagan Penda of Mercia brought about Edwin's defeat in 632. Penda, though an obdurate pagan himself, seems to have been ambivalent in his attitude to missionaries, even permitting his son Peada to receive the new faith. To the Northumbrians he remained the epitome of hostile military power, killing their new king Oswald (later St Oswald) in battle in 641, and finally meeting his own death at the battle of Winwaed in 654 at the hands of Oswald's brother Oswy (641–70). Oswald and Oswy were representatives of the northern group among the Northumbrian peoples, the Bernicians, and they had been brought up in exile during the reign of King Edwin among Celtic Christians based on Iona. Under their protection one of the great figures of the conversion emerged in the person of Abbot Aidan, bishop of Lindisfarne (635–51), by whose inspiration Celtic missionaries spread far and wide among the Germanic kingdoms, preaching and teaching in depth. Bede has harsh things to say about Aidan's imperfect knowledge, which led him to faulty calculations of the proper date of Easter, but has nothing but praise for his way of life, his love of peace and charity, and Christian conduct. Roman-trained missionaries were also active in Wessex and East Anglia, working to all appearances in harmony with the Celts. There was, indeed, no doctrinal difference between the two groups, and the spectre of heresy did not arise. There were, however, conspicuous differences in custom, notably in the matter of dating Easter and also in methods of baptism and the nature of monkish tonsure. Differences of dating could lead to ridiculous situations, where some were celebrating Easter when their husbands or wives or neighbours were still observing the fast of Lent.

After the death of Penda, when all the new kingdoms, except for Sussex, were nominally Christian, these anomalies had to be resolved. At a great synod, held at Whitby in 663 under the presidency of King Oswy himself, a debate was held, and the problems were settled in favour of the Roman cause. Bede has left us a dramatic account of the arguments used, some quite highly technical in relation to the calculations needed to establish the date of Easter. The main political thrust of the Roman case, however, which Bede understood very well, rested on two main interlocking themes: the central authority of Roman tradition as opposed to the insularity of even the holiest among the Celtic saints, and the overpowering majesty of the pope himself, the successor to St Peter. At the climax of the debate King Oswy is said to have asked Colman, the defender of the Celtic cause, if it were true that to St Peter were entrusted the keys of the kingdom of heaven. After Colman's reply that this was indeed so, the king sensibly stated that in that case he was not going to risk offending St Peter. An independent witness, Eddius, a priest of York, records that Oswy was smiling as he asked his question. Iona had nothing to offer that could stand against Rome and access to Mediterranean civilization.

The decisions at Whitby applied initially to Northumbria alone, but in practice involved the triumph of the Roman cause throughout England. The Celtic monks who could not accept the new dispensation withdrew to Iona, but in time all the Celtic communities acquiesced in the up-to-date method of reckoning Easter – the British Christians of Wales not finally until 768. The way was now clear for a period of organization and movement towards unity. A new archbishop of Canterbury was selected, but died in Rome. The pope then, by a masterstroke, appointed a man destined to become one of the great archbishops, Theodore of Tarsus. Already an elderly man of sixty-six at the time of his appointment, he nevertheless held the archiepiscopal office for more than twenty years and, helped by the fine scholar Abbot Adrian, a monk from North Africa, set the new church on a firm institutional footing. He regularized the diocesan system, aiming to establish at least one see for each kingdom, held councils for the whole English church to affirm orthodoxy of belief and establish uniformity of discipline and penance, and fostered intense programmes of education, extending and deepening the use of literacy among the English. In this, the third generation, so to speak, of the conversion period, a great enrichment of intellectual life took place, but political structures were still fragile. The Northumbrian hegemony that had done so much to support the missions collapsed after 685. Wessex under King Ine (688–725) enjoyed a period of stability, but true power began to pass to the lately Christianized Middle Kingdom of Mercia. The kingdoms were still small and disunited, a contrast in so many ways to the ecclesiastical situation, which, by the time of the death of Theodore in 690, showed a precocious English unity.

The effects of ecclesiastical organization were felt throughout the whole of England. By 690 bishoprics existed at Canterbury and Rochester in Kent, at London to serve Middlesex and Essex, at

Dunwich and Elmham in East Anglia, at Winchester in Wessex, at Lichfield, Worcester and Hereford in the West Midlands, and at an uncertain site in the East Midlands, permanently fixed at Leicester in 737. Theodore met resistance from the powerful and turbulent Wilfrid of York in his attempts to rationalize the situation in Northumbria, but bishoprics were set up at Lindisfarne and Hexham as well as York. A separate see was set up for Lindsey. These were all more or less permanent, and arrangements were also made for bishops at Dorchester-on-Thames, Ripon and at Abercorn for the Picts. Sussex was converted, largely by the efforts of St Wilfrid of York, and a bishopric established at Selsey. In the reign of King Ine the great see of Winchester was divided, and a second bishopric placed at Sherborne. The addition of Whithorn in Galloway as a suffragan of York and the elevation of York to archiepiscopal status in 735 completed, with only minor adjustments, the ecclesiastical geography of the English church, which was to survive into the Viking Age. A model of institutional life applicable to the whole English people was provided by the church.

Institutional structures are one thing, the inner life of the church quite another. Support had to be found in the shape of landed endowments and regular offerings for the building and maintenance of churches, the training of the clergy, the provision of schools, and all the apparatus needed for the protection of a clerisy as a class set apart. The laws from the earliest stages show how the Christian church was integrated into the new kingdoms and grew with them. Special *wergelds* protected the bishops and the priests. Churchmen in turn played a vital part in sanctioning oaths and helping to administer the ordeal. Within the short space of less than a century a collection of pagan Germanic kingdoms, driven like a wedge between Celtic Christian communities in the extreme West and the Frankish Christian kingdom on the Continent, had been transformed into a Christianized complex, still diverse politically, but unified religiously and to a large extent socially in their new Christian faith. Saints representing the whole spectrum of Christian experience, from the authoritative and political Wilfrid of York to the withdrawn and savagely ascetic Cuthbert of Lindisfarne, flourished in the milieu.

The success of the conversion was altogether remarkable, though one must be careful not to exaggerate. Our knowledge of it comes primarily, and in some respects almost exclusively, from ecclesiastical sources with an in-built interest in pointing to the completeness of the success. Hints are in fact given of reversion to paganism in times of dearth and trouble, and there was clearly much survival of primitive tendencies to worship groves, streams, ancient holy places and natural phenomena. Such is the characteristic of rural society the world over, and early Anglo-Saxon England was no exception. The reasons for the success are easy to state in general, though again there are complexities when one looks at the situation in depth. Christianity was a mature religion, rooted in the experience of the Mediterranean world, Hebraic, Hellenic, Roman, and above all literate. It was a religion of a great book, the Bible, and also of many books. Literacy gave hopes of permanence and stability. No one should deny, also, the intrinsic strength of a faith that offered direct social teaching in the form of the ten commandments and the Golden Rule of the New Testament, together with a sophisticated theology that placed life in a more rational chronological framework, divine and human.

Yet one should not belittle the pagan presence in early England. There were pagan deities common to the Germanic world, whose names are still embedded in our days of the week; Tiw, Woden, Thor and Freya. There were both pagan priests and high priests; there were pagan festivals, one of which, the spring festival of Eostre, has surprisingly given its name to the most sacred of Christian festivals, Easter. Pagan ritual itself could be elaborate and, if the evidence from the great ship-burial at Sutton Hoo is taken fully into account, such ritual could be both impressive and expensive. At Sutton Hoo, about the year 625 or 626, a warrior-king, probably Redwald of East Anglia, was commemorated by the burial of a ship which carried in its central chamber symbols of royalty, a sceptre-whetstone and standard, precious goods in garnet and gold, jewels of consummate workmanship, and all the apparatus of silver dishes that suggested a ceremonial feast of epic proportions. The ship-burial itself was the most impressive and magnificent element in a high-status (and still mysterious) cemetery, high over the river

Deben in south Suffolk, from which evidence is coming that points to an element of human sacrifice associated with some of the chieftains interred there.

Sutton Hoo came at the very end of the pagan period, just as the missionaries were making headway in East Anglia, and the presence of a pair of christening spoons, inscribed Paul and Saul, gives a clue to the moment of burial in a time of transition from pagan to Christian. Missionaries, acting on the direct instructions of Pope Gregory himself, had been told to handle pagan customs carefully, to use existing holy temples, if appropriate, and to win souls by precept and example rather than force. They seem to have followed such instructions sensibly and well. They aimed to convert the established powers first, the kings, the queens, the royal courts, before moving on to conversion in depth. Such methods contributed greatly to success. The establishments were ripe for conversion; law, literacy, administrative skills followed in the wake of the new faith. One of the most amazing features of the whole story is the absence of martyrs. King Oswald, killed by Penda in 641, was later hailed as a martyr, but he met his death in battle. True martyrs, as we recognize them, are not to be found in seventh-century England, though once the missionaries head for the Continent, in Frisia and Saxony there is quite another story. Insular paganism does not seem to have attracted enough institutional support to lead men to kill the new teachers who dared affront their old traditional beliefs. The weakness of paganism in this sense, coupled with the attractions – political, social and cultural – of the new faith, were enough to ensure the victory for Christianity in a relatively painless and complete fashion.

There are two massive symptoms of success that help to illustrate the point: the phenomenon sometimes described as the Northumbrian Renaissance, and the reverse movement of missionaries back to the Continent, which finally resulted in the conversion of the Germans to the east of the Rhine. For a period of fifty years or so, sometimes called the Age of Bede (672–735) from the name of its greatest scholar, the northern English kingdom became one of the most productive and influential cultural centres of Europe. Its island and coastal sanctuaries at Lindisfarne and the Inner Farne, its religious houses at York, Whitby and Ripon, and above all the twin monastery of Monkwearmouth (founded 673) and Jarrow (681) acquired special fame. These were no weak creations, and their foundation involved a degree of sacrifice and initiative on the part of the kings and the community. When the abbot Ceolfrith set out on his last journey to Rome in June 716, at the age of seventy-four, he left behind him a community reckoned to be six hundred strong. The rules observed by the monks were mixed, though a rule attributed to St Benedict of Nursia was certainly known at Lindisfarne, and some elements of it, relating to the election of abbots, at Monkwearmouth and Jarrow. In the early stages of their existence there is no reason to doubt the substantial integrity of the houses, and it is possible that even now we have not taken fully into account the importance of enforced celibacy upon quite a significant number of intelligent young men and women in assessing the strength and dedication of the cultural life of the times.

The manifestations that still survive are overwhelmingly impressive. Abbot Ceolfrith died on his way to Rome, but the book that he had taken with him as one of his lavish gifts to the pope was delivered after his death; eventually placed in the monastery of Monte Amiata, it has survived to this day in the Laurentian Library in Florence. More than a thousand leaves in length, the so-called Codex Amiatinus is itself a creation of great scribal beauty and has a special place in codicological history as the earliest surviving complete Latin bible. The most famous of all surviving texts, the Lindisfarne Gospels, was made at Lindisfarne about 700, with Bishop Eadfrith responsible for writing the text and possibly responsible himself for the superb illustrations, which still overwhelm the reader by their subtlety of pattern and colour. The Lindisfarne Gospels, written 'for God and St Cuthbert and all the saints whose relics are in the island', ranks among the finest of all books produced during the early Middle Ages – but it does not stand alone. As one of a group of surviving Hiberno-Saxon illuminated gospels, it serves as a sharp reminder of the rich complexity of cultural influences that helped to make Northumbria a special place at this time. Celtic inspiration in artistic forms is coupled with Germanic skill at the zoomorphic decoration and interlace. Strong elements of Italian influence, notably from the south, in the area around Naples, have also been isolated in Northumbrian art. Our terminology itself is inexact and suspect, but within its limitations we can see how the conjunction of Mediterranean, Germanic and Celtic currents flowed successfully into a Northumbrian mainstream. In sculpture and the other arts similar evidence persists. The sculptured crosses at Hexham, Bewcastle and Ruthwell, the Ormside bowl with its classical plant forms, the whalebone Franks casket with scenes from Germanic and Roman legend and runic inscriptions, St Cuthbert's pectoral cross: all indicate artistic output in various media of the very highest quality.

Artistic achievements form the background to a literary revival of the first order. The provision of bibles and gospel books was accompanied by works of commentary, exegesis, telling example, lives of saints and history. In Bede the house of Jarrow and Monkwearmouth contained the greatest scholar of the age. He was born on the estates belonging to the monastery, educated there from the age of seven, first under the tuition of the abbot Benedict Biscop and then Ceolfrith, was made a deacon at nineteen and a priest at thirty. He spent the whole of his life in the monastery and seems never to have moved further than York. His scholarly output was prodigious. We remember him for his *Ecclesiastical History of the English People*, produced late in his life in 731, but a note of his work appended to that history lists twenty-five titles, constituting some sixty books in all. The Latin that he wrote was clear, direct, refreshingly modern in some respects. He was a great communicator and story-teller, using the parable form to maximum effect. He was also a scientist of no mean calibre, deeply involved in, and in the forefront of investigation into the natural sciences and chronology. In his writing he popularized the acceptance of dating from the year of the Incarnation, *anno domini*, AD. He excelled as a commentator on the scriptures, and it was probably in that field rather than for his history that he expected to be remembered. His conception of the true law of history was far ahead of its time, as was also his respect for evidence and his care in assessing information both orally and from writing so that truth could be achieved. His purpose in writing history, the lives of abbots and the *Ecclesiastical History* itself was moral and religious. As he himself declared in his preface to the *Ecclesiastical History*, 'if history relates good things of good men, the attentive hearer is incited to imitate what is good; or if it recounts evil things of wicked persons, nevertheless the devout and godly hearer or reader, shunning that which is hurtful and wrongful, is the more earnestly kindled to perform those things which he knows to be good and worthy of God.' To read, to learn and to teach were Bede's avowed aims in life, and admirably he fulfilled them. He was supreme in his generation, but he was no solitary figure: lives of saints – Cuthbert, Wilfrid and Guthlac – were produced; Bede taught, even providing a grammar for instruction, and there were many pupils. In one of his last letters, in the course of which he expressed his worry about the state of the church in Northumbria, he wrote of the 'innumerable blameless people of chaste conduct, boys and girls, young men and maidens, old men and women, worthy to participate in mass and the sacred mysteries week by week.' He was writing for a Christian audience in a Christian world.

Nor was Northumbria the only kingdom to benefit from the cultural shock administered to pagan peoples by their conversion and subsequent exposure to Mediterranean civilization. The school at Canterbury flourished mightily, and Kent and London continued to receive scholars and books in large numbers direct from the Continent. In Wessex, Aldhelm (639–709), the first bishop of Sherborne, was the most prominent figure, writing in a Latin style that was elaborate and complex, owing much to fashion among the Continental Latinists of his time as well as to Celtic scholarship. The main thrust of scholarly effort was naturally in Latin, but to this period we look for our first knowledge of vernacular poetry devoted to Christian ends. Caedmon at Whitby, in the later years of the rule of the Abbess Hilda (614–80), composed poetry on religious themes, calculated to bring people to a deeper understanding of the faith. From the cultural point of view, as it impinged on the religious, the conversion of the English to Christianity was one of the most successful missionary movements of all time: indirectly it served to create a special English identity.

A further pointer to the vitality of the new Christian communities comes from our knowledge of the missionary efforts that they themselves conducted back into the Continent. As early as 677 St Wilfrid, on his way to Rome to appeal against Archbishop Theodore's schemes for reorganization, had preached the faith in Frisia, but it was another decade and more before systematic efforts could be made to convert the still heathen Germans to the east of the Rhine, notably the Frisians and the Old Saxons. Political and ecclesiastical motives converged to give muscle to the enterprise. After 687 and his victory at Tertry, Pippin, mayor of the palace in Austrasia and ancestor of Charlemagne, founded what was in essentials a new ruling dynasty among the Franks. It was in his interests, as also in the interest of the papacy, that Christian communities should exist on his eastern frontier. For the following century and right through to the forced conversion of the Old Saxons in the reign of Charlemagne, intense missionary efforts were directed against the Continental Germans, and English missionaries, speaking a language closely akin to the people they were called on to convert, played a major part in the enterprise. Willibrord, whose most effective work was done among the Frisians from his main base near Utrecht, was the principal figure in the early stages of a long mission that lasted from 695, when he received a papal commission, to the time of his death at Echternach in 739. He was a Northumbrian and so were all the early English missionaries.

In the second decade of the eighth century a further change came over affairs with the beginning of the mission of one of the great men of the age: Winfrith, St Boniface of Crediton in Devon (675–755), a West Saxon, trained at Exeter and at the monastic house of Nursling in Hampshire. Frankish military support and papal sanction characterized his work as much as Willibrord's, but his range was much more extensive, and his success stupendous. Made bishop to the Germans by Pope Gregory II in 722 and archibishop by Gregory III in 732, he established his permanent cathedral at Mainz in 747. By that time he had truly become the Apostle to the Germans, reorganizing or founding dioceses along the border, dividing the new and fragile Bavarian church into sees at Salzburg, Regensburg, Freising, Passau and Eichstatt, and establishing new sees, some under the control of Englishmen, notably at Würzburg and Erfurt.

With enormous prestige behind him, he was also instrumental in carrying through reforms to the Frankish church itself and played a prominent part in what proved to be the most significant political move of the age, the removal of the Merovingian dynasty and the recognition of the Frankish mayor, Pippin le Bref, as Christian king of the Franks. His last mission, again to the Frisians in 755, ended in failure, massacre and martyrdom, but the positive results of his career proved enduring.

Not least among these, and vital as an element in the making of the English nation, was the effect of his work on his homeland. Indeed, it is hard to overestimate the impact of his particular ventures. Sharing a great enterprise does more than anything else to bring people together, and Boniface received active support in men, money, moral and spiritual comfort from all the kingdoms of England. Women were prominent among his helpers as nuns and abbesses. The traditions of the English church, where women from princesses to formidable abbesses and humble nuns were prominent from the earliest stages, were carried forward into the mission and did much to foster a sense of oneness among the insular peoples. It is at this time that the expression 'Anglo-Saxon' appears to have been used of the Germanic inhabitants of England to distinguish them from the Continental Old Saxons, a delicate pointer to the unity achieved in religious fields long before political unification became possible. In return for the support received, Boniface was lavish in his advice and admonition to the communities back home. He wrote in powerful Latin, and a mass of his correspondence has survived, especially his letters to the papal court. Enough also has survived from England to show that he operated in a literate world in the full sense of the term. It so happens that most of his correspondence came from the south and serves as a reminder of the strength of eighth-century Kentish and West Saxon education, but the school at York still remained famous, and its library prestigious.

The flourishing of fine churches, such as Brixworth in Northamptonshire, the evolution of schools of ecclesiastical sculpture in the East Midlands, the vernacular poetry of Cynewulf, provide the background to Boniface's zeal and enterprise. England was a community from which he could draw books and art, as well as men and women; and the impact of such gifts proved permanent on the German scene. Germany benefited from intense contact with new, vigorous Christian impulses from the insular Anglo-Saxons at a critical moment, when Frankish political dominance was bringing it firmly into the political structures of a new empire, which, with the coronation of Charlemagne at Rome in 800, was to reshape the life of Western Christendom. Boniface did not hesitate to upbraid rulers and prominent churchmen if he thought they were failing in duties that involved the maintenance of a Christian moral order, or inadequate in their support of the holding of church councils of reform. On moral questions he was firm, castigating immorality and drunkenness (a special English affliction) even among the highest in the land. In a famous letter to Ethelbald of Mercia (716–57), the strongest ruler of the day, Boniface did not pull his punches. Joined by seven other missionary bishops, all his subordinates, he urged Ethelbald to moral reform and to resist despoiling the church, lest 'the whole people, sinking to lower and baser things, will finally neither be strong in secular warfare, nor stable in faith, neither honoured by men nor loved by God.' Active missionaries were well placed, drawing awful examples from Spain, Provence or the Burgundian peoples, to exhort rulers to remember their duties as Christian kings.

For a generation after Boniface's death English missionaries continued to be active, but English influence switched in the second half of the eighth century away from the mission field to the study, a tribute in itself to the success of the process of conversion. Bede's pupil Egbert, archibishop of York (735–66), and his successor Ethelbert (767–80) created at York one of the great European libraries and centres of scholarship. Alcuin (735–804), the most distinguished product of the school, left a poem on the saints of York that suggests a library strong on patristic literature and Christian poetry, though weak on classical texts. The career of Alcuin itself tells us much of the status of English scholarship and so of the English peoples. An outstanding young scholar, he appears to have been substantially in charge of the library and the school during Ethelbert's early years as archbishop, actively involved with the Frisian mission and twice undertaking the journey to Rome. In 782 he was persuaded by Charlemagne to join the group of scholars at the royal court at Aix-la-Chapelle and became virtually head of the school there, attracting other Englishmen to the Carolingian court. Greatly influential in theological and intellectual matters, he was prominent in revising the text of the Vulgate, and served as a key adviser on all matters of diplomatic and political problems. As a letter-writer he was supreme, and his letters were collected in the ninth century to serve as examples of the epistolary art to future generations. It is ironic that three of the most influential Englishmen of the whole period, Bede, St Boniface and Alcuin, flourished in the eighth century, which scarcely ranks among the most interesting or best-known centuries in English medieval history.

The career of Alcuin takes us away from the problems of conversion to a world that had been converted. We shall have to consider his work later in relation to King Offa and Charlemagne. In a well-known letter to King Ethelred of Northumbria he lamented the attack of the Vikings on Lindisfarne in 793. As a proem to the substance of the letter he gave what he considered to be the true context in which to regard it, a context that involved a patristic attitude to royal government and the community. It incorporates much Augustinian thought, as transmitted by Pope Gregory, and to quote it gives as good an indication as any of the success of the conversion and of the complex manner in which the concept of Christian kingship helped to point the way towards the creation of a more rational order. 'We are citizens', wrote Alcuin, 'of the same country, and therefore I do not cease to warn you of the things known to belong to the welfare of an earthly kingdom and to the beatitude of an eternal kingdom . . . To what does a man owe fidelity, if not to his fatherland? To whom does he owe prosperity, if not to its citizens? We are fellow-citizens by a two-fold relationship: sons of one city in Christ, that is of Mother Church, and natives of one country.' Such high theory seemed often far from brutal reality, but carried on by a literate minority, the idea of effective kingship, buttressed and yet disciplined by a Christian faith, offered hope for the creation of a polity that could incorporate peacefully the English nation.

CHAPTER 3

Political consolidation: c. 700–975

The changes that came over Western Europe between 700 and 975 were deep, dramatic and far-reaching. In the economic and social fields final steps were taken in the transformation of what was still in 700 essentially a sub-Roman, classical, Mediterranean-based world into a medieval, land-based, Germano-Romanic world where the plough was king, and in which the axis of political power swung north and east, away from the Mediterranean and towards the Carolingian heartlands of Lorraine and Aix-la-Chapelle. The Moslems invaded and conquered the greater part of Spain in the first two decades of the eighth century. They threatened the very existence of Constantinople itself, and, though in 717 their greatest effort against the city failed, their soldiers and sailors and religion were left dominant over most of the Near East, all of the North African littoral, and most of the Mediterranean waters. The shrunken, landlocked world of Rome and the West found some compensation for loss in the slow conversion and absorption of the Continental Germans. Charlemagne, crowned and hailed as Augustus at Rome by Pope Leo III on Christmas Day 800, provided in his empire, his *imperium Christianum*, as some called it, a feeling of political integrity to the new groupings of peoples in what can now properly be called Western civilization. The English kingdoms were not within that empire, but they were intimately connected with it and affected by it. Indeed, because of these tremendous realignments on a world scale, England was called on to play a more vital role in Western affairs, and could no longer be regarded as part of a remote island far removed from the mainstream of events. In this context English moves towards political unity take on quite a new significance.

The English church, as we have seen, played a major role in the conversion of the Continental Germans. The martyrdom of St Boniface at the hands of the Frisians at Dokkum in 755 marked a dramatic phase in that process, isolating the Continental Saxons and Frisians in their paganism, in marked contrast to the Christian Germans of the southern and central Germanic lands. By the end of the century English scholars, notably Alcuin of York, were providing a strong element in the royal Frankish educational policy centred on the palace school at Aix. In this new Carolingian phase in European development the English kingdoms offer something of a mirror to developments in the empire itself and to the successor divisions of the empire, which by 950 had taken on recognizable shape as the kingdoms of France and Germany.

Politically, the period falls into two principal sections, with a curious indeterminate phase in the middle of the ninth century. From the second or third decade of the eighth century to the time of the death of King Offa in 796, and in some measure through to 825, the main power in England was the Middle Kingdom of Mercia. After the defeat of the Mercian King Beornwulf at the hands of King Egbert of Wessex in 825, Wessex was plainly in the ascendant, but the full effects of the defeat were not experienced until later in the century, and then only under the completely new circumstances created by the full-scale Viking attacks. Scandinavian pirates had raided English coasts in the last decades of the eighth century, and on 8 June 793, as the Anglo-Saxon Chronicle reported it, 'the ravages of heathen men miserably destroyed God's church on Lindisfarne with plunder and slaughter.' Alcuin, writing from the security of the Frankish court, was deeply shaken by this fearsome act, not least because of its completely unexpected nature. Viking mastery of ship-building techniques, which made navigation in northern waters an acceptable risk, brought a new element into the political life of north-west Europe. In the early years of the ninth century Scandinavians settled permanently in the Northern Islands, Orkney and Shetland. They set up their fortified staging posts and markets in Ireland in the 830s, and in 851 they made their first abortive attempt at settlement in England, in the Isle of Thanet. In the 860s, a decade of intense Scandinavian activity throughout the whole of the civilized world, they started their serious attempts at conquest and settlement.

From 865 for the best part of a century to 954, English political history was dominated by the need to defeat and contain the Danes. The inspired leadership of a remarkable dynasty, King Alfred (871–99), his son Edward the Elder (899–924) and grandson Athelstan (924–39), met this need, and in so doing ensured that Wessex emerged as the dominant Christian kingdom of England, the basis for the unitary kingdom over all England. The well-known and dramatic contribution of the West Saxons to English unity should not, however, obscure the earlier achievements of the Mercians, and we must first, in any attempt to reach a rounded picture, look carefully at the permanent effect of the century of Mercian dominance. Northumbria, in spite of the precocious vitality of the kingdom in the seventh century, had failed to maintain its leading position in English affairs. Poor communications, deep tensions between the prosperous Deira, the Vale of York, and harsh Bernicia, Pictish revival and insistent Mercian hostility all contributed to its political downfall. The eighth century turned out to be a sad time for the Northumbrians, except in the literary field, where the school of York, with its impressive library and galaxy of scholars, continued to flourish. Pictish resurgence brought all hopes of further expansion to an end and even placed control of Lothian in peril. Internal violence and feuding exaggerated the basic weakness caused by the divergent interests of Deira and Bernicia. The Mercians were ready poised to take advantage of the situation. As so often happens in these centuries, their initial political success generated its own impetus, and the Mercians moved forward to increasing cumulative achievements until, in the early ninth century, the impetus gave out.

Two kings dominated the English scene in the eighth century, both of them Mercian: Ethelbald (716–57) and Offa (757–96). Both were formidable warriors – and, indeed, the military flavour to Mercian overlordship has led to a belittlement of its final achievement. Modern investigation is beginning to redress the balance, and we now recognize the eighth century as a vital phase in the creation of settled communities in England. Archaeologists, putting together scattered and difficult evidence, find traces of a considerable shift in settlement patterns; place-name experts looking in depth at the complexities of our common names, notably those compounded with '-ton', begin to establish a realistic general chronology; attempts to synthesize, no matter how tentative, tend to regard the eighth century as formative in stabilizing the agrarian settlement of much of England. In social terms the inference is clear, pointing to a decisive move from lordship to landlordship, from a dominant kindred element to a territorial in determining relationships of lords to men.

The principal landmarks in the poorly recorded reign of Ethelbald are precise, though the steps by which his success was achieved are uncertain. By 731 he controlled all England south of the Humber, and Bede enumerated the provinces subject to him: Kent, Essex, East Anglia, Wessex, Mercia itself, Hereford and Worcester (the province of Hwicce), the Isle of Wight. Bede is thinking at this stage in terms of bishoprics, and his summing-up, that 'all these provinces and the other southern provinces as far as the boundary formed by the river Humber' lie under Ethelbald's authority, conceals a great variety in lordship. Wessex maintained a degree of independence, though charters show Ethelbald giving the Berkshire monastery of Cookham to Christ Church, Canterbury. Although the missionaries, notably St Boniface, railed at the immorality of the royal court, Ethelbald was a benefactor to the church, concerned with reform. He exercised firm control over London, while his general achievement was to weld together the Middle Kingdom into a strong political unit, drawing on the growing arable resources of the Midland Plain. He dealt with communities used to the imposition of taxes, and it seems very likely that it was during his reign that the process of exacting systematic fyrd-service was applied to all landed estates not specifically exempt. Even so, his reign ended in violence; a defeat at the hands of the West Saxons in 752 and a palace revolution in 757 led to his murder. After a short, troubled period he was succeeded by one of the greatest of the early Anglo-Saxon kings, Offa, who completed and extended his achievements. Offa's contribution to the making of England was considerable; he was the strongest ruler in the island for some forty years.

1   Bede, from a twelfth-century version of his Life of St Cuthbert.

2　Back panel of the Franks Casket at the British Museum, illustrating the siege of Jerusalem in AD 70. Whalebone. Northumbrian Renaissance.

3　The basic element of the sceptre-whetstone of the Sutton Hoo ship-burial, a symbol of pagan royalty. A ring and bronze stag surmounted the stone sceptre.

4　Christening spoons from the Sutton Hoo ship-burial, inscribed Paul and Saul: a conversion symbol in a pagan setting.

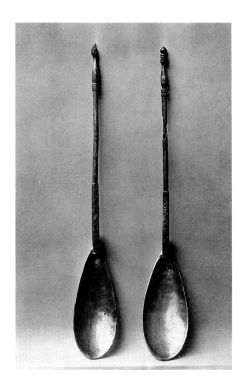

5   Decorated initial from the Gospel of St Matthew. Lindisfarne Gospels. *Christi autem generatio sic erat . . .*

6   Splendid carpet-page illustration from the Lichfield Gospels, second quarter of the eighth century.

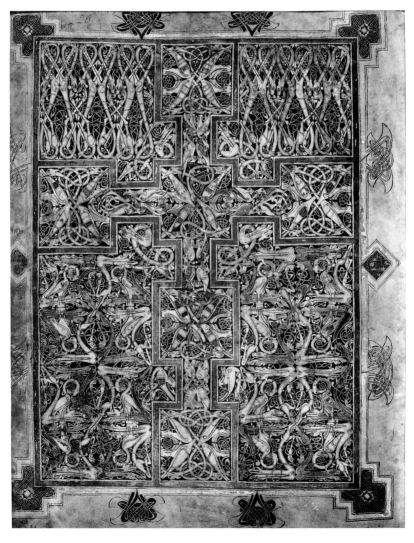

7   Panel from St Cuthbert's coffin, Durham, late seventh century. The figure of Christ.

8, 9   The stole of St Cuthbert, Durham, showing St Peter and Jonah. Winchester work of the early tenth century, presented to the shrine by King Athelstan in 934.

10   Frontispiece of the Codex Amiatinus, Florence. Ezra at work at the sacred
texts. Northumbrian Renaissance.

11 The island of
Iona, base from which
Celtic missionaries
operated in the
seventh-century
conversion of the
English to Christianity.

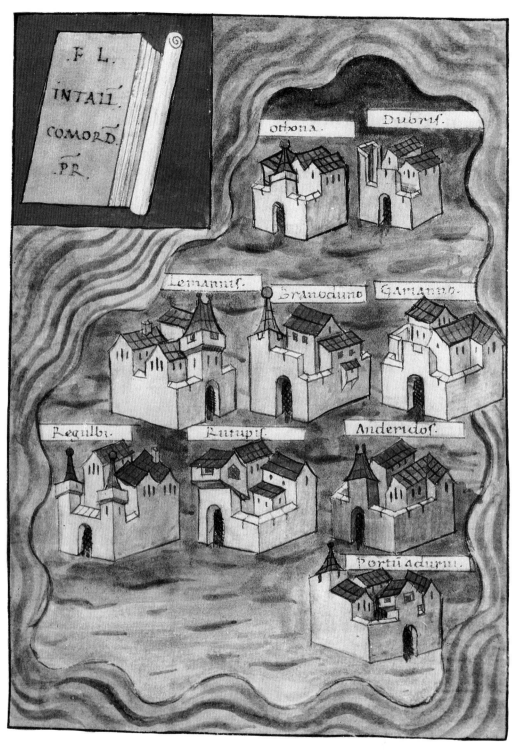

12 The forts of the Saxon shore – *Othona* (Bradwell-on-Sea) and Dover on top, Portchester on the bottom line – from a fifteenth-century manuscript, copied from a Carolingian version of the fourth-century *Notitia Dignitatum*.

At this time political institutions throughout the West were undergoing momentous change. Offa was a contemporary of the Frankish ruler Charlemagne, king of the Franks 768–814 and emperor from 800. The Mercian was indeed the one Western king able to meet with Charles on terms of a rough equality in status, king to king. Both men, in their respective spheres and differing contexts, illustrate an increasing note of professionalism in the Christian kings of Western Europe.

Offa's conspicuous achievements lie in the political and military fields. Chronicle evidence is patchy, but charter evidence demonstrates that he was able spasmodically to grant lands in Kent without reference to Kentish kings, and that he confirmed land grants in Sussex both before and after his conquest of those who dwelt around Hastings in 771. He kept a firm and watchful eye on Wessex, winning a battle at Bensington in 779 and influencing dynastic affairs by a successful marriage policy. The young West Saxon prince Egbert was forced into what was eventually to turn out to be a profitable exile in Carolingian Frankia. Within the bounds of the Middle Kingdom itself prestigious families with virtual dynastic rights over regions were converted into subordinate ealdormen. The rulers of the Hwicce, that is to say the men settled around Worcester, subscribed to early charters as *reguli* (rulers), but by the middle of Offa's reign as *subreguli*, a term best rendered *ealdormen*. Indeed, Offa seems to have followed a deliberate policy of depreciation in status for all kingdoms south of the Humber, though to the north he contented himself with occasional punitive raids against the Northumbrians. Late in his reign Offa extended his authority vigorously to the east. The ancient dynasty of independent rulers of East Anglia was represented in the early 790s by a young and handsome king, Ethelbert by name. In a crime that captured the imagination of later generations Offa had the young king killed when he was on a friendly visit to Offa's court arranging a marriage to Offa's daughter. The great abbey of St Albans was founded in atonement for the deed, and attempts, notably by St Albans writers, to whitewash Offa and to place the blame on his queen, Cynethryth, do not ring true. A folk-cult developed around Ethelbert, who was regarded as a saint. Hereford cathedral, the nearest great church to the scene of his death at Sutton Walls, was later dedicated to St Ethelbert, king and martyr.

The absorption of East Anglia by force completed the consolidation of the native Germanic kingdoms south of the Humber. London became to all intents and purposes a Mercian city, a point of greater importance than we have yet realized. In a sense this was a fitting reward for the military prowess of Offa, who had proved able to give a rough but effective protection to the Southumbrians. His power of command and also, perhaps, his diplomatic skill are best illustrated by the great dyke that still bears his name in both English and Welsh, Offa's dyke, *clawdd Offa*, the boundary between the English and the Welsh. Although not all Welshmen lived to the west of the dyke and not all Englishmen to the east, it has been customary to regard the dyke as an agreed frontier between the two peoples. Modern investigation suggests that this is not an accurate view, that military purpose was the chief reason for construction, and that the great work, topped by a stone wall in places, ran continuously (apart from relatively short sections where rivers served as effective markers) for the whole 150 miles or so from sea to sea, probably from Basingwerk to near Chepstow. It was a massive work, one of the great European archaeological monuments. The sheer logistics involved in the recruitment of labour and the ability to keep the labourers hard at work for what must surely have been decades are reminders of the authority of the Mercian king. Offa's dyke should not be envisaged as a sort of Hadrian's Wall, permanently manned, strictly controlling ingress and egress of even small groups of people. It served a useful purpose for many centuries, deep into the central Middle Ages, as a territorial demarcation of a legal boundary between those who were governed by English law and those by Welsh, and as a physical deterrent to cattle-raiding.

Offa's position was so powerful that he could treat realistically on the international stage. With Charlemagne his relationship varied from co-operation in ecclesiastical affairs and the movement of pilgrims, to negotiations of some positive advantage but also considerable turbulence over trade and marriage arrangements. Papal legates visited England in 786 and, at a great council held by Offa, accompanied by the West Saxon king Cynewulf, issued reforming decrees – afterwards moving on to the Northumbrians at York. The international prestige implied in such activity is the external symbol of Mercian success, and we are increasingly aware of the internal advances made towards English unity in the eighth century. There is marked contrast between the overlordship exercised by Ethelbald and Offa, and that enjoyed by the most powerful rulers in the preceding century, who had been essentially leaders of federations, owing their dignity to military authority exercised against the British. The number of kingdoms in England did not diminish in the seventh century, but Mercian kingship was different, in a sense all-absorbing, and institutional growth took place to meet the new demands, in particular of Offa's reinforced Christian kingship.

From Carolingian sources Offa drew inspiration for strengthening his dynasty; he had his son Ecgfrith consecrated in his own lifetime with the aim of avoiding succession problems. He was careful in his handling of the church. The legatine visitation of 786–7 was clearly prompted by Offa and his advisers with the triple object of stimulating reform, sanctioning legitimate dynastic succession to the kingdom and also setting up a new archbishopric at Lichfield. The experiment failed at Lichfield; Hygebald, the first and last archbishop, held office until his death in 803, but that was that; the prestige of Canterbury was too deep-rooted. Church reform was a different matter: councils were held under royal supervision and drawn from all England. The repercussions on the king's court were considerable. Regular meetings of the wise men – the *witan*, or *seniores* – were held, consisting of the king, his advisers, chief thegns and ealdormen, and ecclesiastics from all over the country. The king's style became more precise, not only king of the Mercians, but on some occasions king of the English, and in one document at least as *rex totius Anglorum patriæ*: king of all the homeland of the English. The coinage was reformed, initially independently in Kent under the influence of trade with Frankia in the later 770s, but quickly extending under royal direction to the greater Mercian kingdom. Coins of high quality and beautiful workmanship were struck, silver pennies that normally now bore the king's name and title. Offa's pennies, similar to the deniers of Carolingian Frankia, and inspired by them but superior in execution and craftsmanship, set the general pattern for English currency over the succeeding five centuries. Coins were also issued in the name of Queen Cynethryth and of the archbishop of Canterbury.

The issue of charters granting land to laymen as well as to clerics became more common, and the diplomatic uses within the charters more sophisticated. It was during the eighth century that the formula was adopted known to scholars as the *trinoda necessitas* – that is to say the threefold necessity that remained as public obligation on virtually all land: the duty to serve in the army, or *fyrd*, the duty to help with the maintenance of fortifications, and the duty to see to the preservation and good repair of bridges. It is probable that insistence on fyrd-duty anticipated the other two, and was placed among the normal reservations in charter grants by the middle of the century. It is a mark of an organized community that landowners should recognize their communal obligations to defence against outside enemies and ease of communications within. By the end of the reign of Offa great advance had been made towards the creation of a coherent community.

Offa deserves praise for his permanent institutional creations, but there were also serious criticisms to be made, which contemporaries or near-contemporaries were quick to voice. Much Mercian achievement depended in the last resort on brute force. The men of Kent and of East Anglia were alienated by Offa's harsh rule. Religious susceptibilities of the southerners, especially at Canterbury, were affronted by the creation of the archbishopric at Lichfield. Offa's son Ecgfrith, duly selected and consecrated as his father's successor, outlived his father by only five months, and his premature death was regarded by many as retribution for Offa's severity. Cenwulf, a distant cousin, succeeded (796–823), and, though he was no mere cipher, Kentish revolts weakened him and his control of Kent became increasingly remote. He could not re-establish the position held by Offa, was unable to prevent the exiled Egbert from assuming the West Saxon throne in 802, and was either too weak or too sensible to continue the Lichfield archiepiscopate. Succession difficulties accelerated the decline of Mercia in the 820s, by which time Egbert of Wessex had quietly consolidated his position in the south-west. In 815 there is record of a serious ravaging expedition in Cornwall from east to west. Decisive political changes came about as a result of successful battles between West Saxons and Mercians in 825 and again in 829.

West Saxon victory at *Ellendun* (Wroughton in Wiltshire to the south of Swindon) put an end to Mercian hopes of supremacy. The men of Kent, Surrey, Sussex and Essex turned to the West Saxon king, and the defeated Mercian king Beornwulf was killed by the East Angles, who appealed to Egbert for protection because of their fear of the Mercians. Mercia itself was conquered in 829, and the Northumbrians were compelled to offer Egbert submission and peace. Such extensive authority did not prove immediately long-lasting, as independent rulers re-emerged in Mercia. But the Anglo-Saxon Chronicle hailed Egbert as the eighth of the *bretwaldas* (rulers of Britain), linking him with the imperial war leaders of the seventh century and earlier. His last campaigns were fought in 838 in Cornwall against Scandinavian pirates assisted by Cornishmen. The south-east remained firmly within the orbit of the revived West Saxon monarchy; Egbert made a reality of political control south of the Thames from Kent to Cornwall. When his son Ethelwulf, a ruler already accustomed to royal responsibilities in the south-east, succeeded his father in 839, the shape of historic England was beginning clearly to emerge.

The period that ran roughly from the middle years of the ninth century to the death of King Edgar in 975 was a time of vital importance in the making of the English nation. Two interlocking themes pervade it: the advent and settlement of a significant population of Scandinavians, especially Danes, and the consolidation of the position of the West Saxon dynasty as the leaders and the symbols of a new united Christian English kingdom. These themes can and should be read as a localized insular expression of a general European phenomenon. Barbarian invasions – Magyar, Moslem and Slav as well as Scandinavian – brought disruption and misery to the greater part of the Carolingian empire. Recovery came slowly with the growth of feudal institutions and the emergence of royal dynasties – the Saxon house in Germany after 919, the Capetians in France after 987 – which were able to organize effective local defence against swift-moving, devastating marauders. Slowly the barbarians were contained, Christianized and absorbed, in the Danelaw in England after 878, as in Normandy in France after 911. The House of Wessex acquitted itself well and, by the reign of Edgar (959–75), was poised to make fresh advance towards a coherent English monarchy.

The kingdom of Wessex enjoyed one outstanding advantage in the peculiar political conditions of the ninth century, and that was its geographical position to the south of the British Isles. Though it suffered severely from Danish raiding, and no part of it was completely free from occasional ravaging by freebooters who came by sea or by land, the main Scandinavian urge towards settlement came from different directions. For simple reasons of transport and logistics, the colonizing effort in the main Danish move was directed against Northumbria, East Anglia and Eastern Mercia, using the migrant points of entry to the fertile, cereal-bearing lands of the east through the Humber and its tributaries and through the Wash. The Scandinavians, Norwegians as well as Danes, looked for two principal conditions for their permanent settlements. The first of these was the existence of reasonable arable and pasture in communities where they could achieve complete political control, or where land was available and military resistance weak. The second was land where they could exploit their capacity to set up fortified markets, preferably on terms with, and with the active connivance of at least an influential part of the indigenous population.

Ireland offered classic examples for the setting up of fortified markets in Dublin, Waterford, Wexford and Limerick. The Northern Isles, Orkney, Shetland up to the Faroes, Iceland and Greenland offered virtually fresh colonizing prospects. The Danelaw in eastern England, Lancashire and the north-west in the early tenth century, and to some extent the Hebrides and the Western Isles down to the Isle of Man, all offered, with varying tempo, hopes of permanent settlement where there was little effective political resistance after the initial impetus. Wessex stood outside these patterns. Not only was she relatively remote geographically, but she proved able to offer tough and continuous military resistance. The number of Scandinavian migrants was not inexhaustible, and the main stock was absorbed elsewhere in the north and east of England.

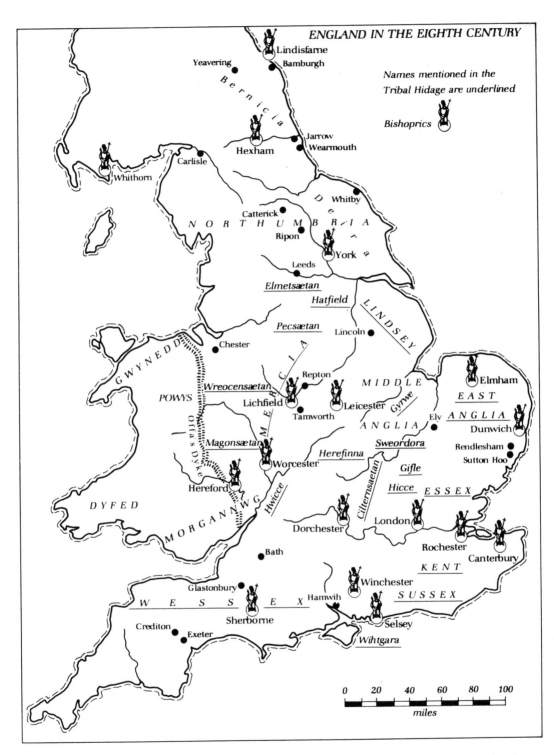

ENGLAND IN THE EIGHTH CENTURY

Names mentioned in the
Tribal Hidage are underlined

Bishoprics

Lindisfarne
Bamburgh
Yeavering
Bernicia
Jarrow
Wearmouth
Hexham
Carlisle
Whithorn
Deira
Whitby
NORTHUMBRIA
Catterick
Ripon
York
Leeds
Elmetsaetan
Hatfield
LINDSEY
Pecsaetan
Lincoln
GWYNEDD
Chester
MERCIA
MIDDLE
Elmham
POWYS
Repton
Leicester
Gyrwe
EAST
ANGLIA
Wreocensaetan
Lichfield
Tamworth
ANGLIA
Dunwich
Offa's Dyke
Magonsaetan
Worcester
Herefinna
Sweordora
Rendlesham
Sutton Hoo
Ely
Gifle
Hereford
Hicce
ESSEX
DYFED
Ciltemsaetan
Hwicce
Dorchester
London
Rochester
MORGANNWG
Canterbury
Bath
KENT
Glastonbury
Winchester
WESSEX
Hamwih
SUSSEX
Crediton
Sherborne
Selsey
Exeter
Wihtgara

0   20   40   60   80   100
miles

Not all places mentioned in the Tribal Hidage have been identified but an accurate up-to-date list
(including locations for many small Fenland folk such as the Bilmiga and the Widerigga) is given by
David Hill, Atlas of Anglo-Saxon England, p.76-7. Syddensis civitas, the seat of the bishop of Lindsey,
has not been identified.

Wessex had other advantages. She enjoyed good communications and, on the whole, willing subjects or potential subjects in the south-east. London retained its links with Mercia, but as its defence came to rest on the West Saxons, moved naturally into the new but still Christian orbit against the heathen invaders. The fortunes of war played their part. In the event, the West Saxon rulers, of the House of Cerdic, proved to be the only ancient English dynasty to survive the Scandinavian onslaught. This is no place for a long narrative account of the Danish wars, but the main outlines should be in our minds as we discuss the West Saxon achievement. The dynasty was lucky in producing the right men at the right time. About some of them, notably Alfred the Great (871–99) and Athelstan (924–39), we are well informed. Others, such as the enigmatic Edward the Elder (899–924), remain mysterious. All contributed at critical times to the making of the English nation, while the ancillary royal figures Aethelflaed, Lady of the Mercians, Alfred's daughter and Edward's sister, and a succession of royal princes and ealdormen helped to give not merely a personal but also a dynamic leadership to the English Christians.

The main Danish onslaught began in 865. East Anglia, Northumbria and Eastern Mercia, north and east of Watling Street, were overrun in the course of the following decade, but the young Alfred, neither too gloriously nor too certainly, managed to buy and sustain a period of peace for Wessex. His full testing time came in the late 870s. For a brief period in 878 he was driven back into the fastnesses of the Somerset marshes at Athelney, while the Danes more or less ravaged at will. The victory of the Devonshire ealdorman Odda, at Countisbury Hill, protected the western shires, but the central heartlands of Wessex suffered severely, and there was even talk of mass migration out of England. Alfred's emergence from Athelney, when his thegns rejoiced in him, and his victory at Edington saved the day. The Danish leader Guthrum accepted terms and was converted to Christianity. The Danes recoiled from Wessex and Western Mercia.

In 886 Alfred occupied London, placing it under the authority of Ethelred, a Mercian ealdorman and Alfred's son-in-law, married to his brave and able daughter Aethelflaed. The last great Danish onslaught in the 890s was repulsed, and the Anglo-Saxon Chronicle could report in 896 that the Danish army divided, one force going into East Anglia, one into Northumbria, while those that were without resources got themselves ships and went south across the sea to the Seine. The chronicler could rejoice that 'by the grace of God the army had not on the whole afflicted the English people very greatly'. Alfred died in 899, still a comparatively young man in his early fifties. His achievements won applause from later historians. Alone among English kings he is known as the Great.

Alfred's reputation deservedly stands high, and from our point of view, concerned with the making of the English nation, there is much to commend that judgment. Alfred's resistance to the Danes was heroic and successful, the stuff from which national legends could be woven. It should be remembered, however, that to a Northumbrian, an East Angle and to many Mercians, the last quarter of the ninth century must have appeared a time of almost unrelieved disaster. The Danish invasion and migration had been contained, but it had also been successful. More than half of Christian England, along the line of the river Lea from just east of London to Bedford and then along Watling Street towards Chester, remained in the hands of Scandinavians who were either heathen or precariously Christianized. The Danelaw covered something like half of England. From the Continent the position looked bleak, and Pope Formosus wrote in the 890s to express concern at the lack of progress in converting the heathen and deep anxiety over the state of episcopal succession.

Yet positive achievements had also been made and proved permanent. Alfred had preserved and reinforced his little Christian kingdom, which was strong enough and sufficiently well-organized to serve as a springboard towards the creation of a kingdom of England. His personality contributed a great deal to this end. He was a devout supporter of the church. His attitude to government was Christian and Carolingian. In spite of the constant military threats, he found time to frame laws that were meant to apply to all Christian peoples under his control. In the preface to his legal code he set out what amounted to a legal philosophy based on the New Testament and his own reading of history. Men were instructed to judge fairly, to make sure that they judged to no man what they would not be judged to them. Alfred was hesitant about making new law, because he had no knowledge of what would be pleasing in turn to his successors. But he had great respect for old law and selected that which was most just from the laws of Ine of the West Saxons, Offa of the Mercians and Ethelbert of Kent. Mercians and men of Kent could indeed feel that the mantle of their ancient dynasties had fallen on this Christian king. He was sensitive to Mercian feelings in other ways. A coin issued soon after 886 shows him as king over both communities with the significant inscription 'Alfred, *rex Angl[orum]*'. There was conscious policy behind this search for wider sanction for kingship.

In the administrative fields permanent advance was also made. Alfred reorganized the defence of his kingdom in a manner patient of further extension as his range widened. He provided a network of fortified points, called *burhs*, around greater Wessex, maintained by an extension of traditional Anglo-Saxon taxation systems. Obligation to defend the *burhs* fell on surrounding landlords, whose estates, assessed in hides, were empowered to provide so many men for the defence of the walls of the *burh* at a set ratio of provision of 16 men for every 22 yards. At Cricklade, for example, there were 1500 hides in support, enough to supply 1500 men and to cover defence and maintenance of some $2062\frac{1}{2}$ yards, which roughly corresponds to the circuit of the earthwork defences. Similar correspondence with known circuits occurs in relation to Winchester, Wareham, Bath, Malmesbury, Wallingford, Lyng, Southampton and Portchester. Our information, which comes from a document dating from Edward the Elder's reign, seems to be accurate and to describe a realistic means of defending and paying for *burhs*, permanent defensive posts against barbarian attack. Most of them developed into boroughs, a word derived of course from the Anglo-Saxon *burh*. The success of the system was shown in the Danish wars of the 890s and was capable of extension elsewhere. It was also linked in Alfred's day with a successful reorganization of the *fyrd* into two sections, one at home and the other out on expedition, apart from those men specifically empowered to defend the *burhs*. The ealdormen, who were the chief of the king's men in the shires, played an increasingly active part in supervising defence, presiding over shire courts and generally controlling the thegnage, who were responsible for active leadership in the field. The authority of secular lords increased under pressure of circumstances, but was not allowed to grow out of hand. In a kingdom that was not too big to manage, Alfred and his ealdormen, thegns and reeves actively canalized the energies of the community into successful defence against the heathen. Even when his experiments did not prove too successful, as in his naval ventures, when his ships proved too cumbersome and ran aground, one is aware of a lively controlling intelligence at work.

Support of the church and learning was part of the fabric of Alfred's kingship. The king himself deliberately embarked on an educational policy, helped by scholars drawn from Western Mercia, Wales, Flanders and Continental Saxony. He took part in an elaborate programme of translation from Latin to Anglo-Saxon, with the object of making those books 'most necessary for all men to know' more generally available. He set out his reasons for doing so in his preface to the translation of Pope Gregory's *Pastoral Care*, in itself a potent treatise on the exercise of authority:

> We can very easily with God's help, if we have the peace, bring it to pass that all the youth now in England, born of free men who have the means that they can apply to it, may be devoted to learning as long as they cannot be of use in any other employment until such a time as they can read well what is written in English. One can then teach further in the Latin language those whom one wishes to teach further and to bring to holy orders.

There were social and political reasons behind this concern with education: an awareness of the need for a disciplined population in the face of a heathen peril. Alfred played the part, on a much smaller scale, of a Charlemagne, a theocrat, harnessing the loyalties of the church and of secular lordship to the Christian community of England.

Alfred's successors completed his work, reabsorbing into Christian England the territories that had passed under Scandinavian control. This was a complicated business not to be read in terms of simple military conquest. Danish farmers who accepted Christianity proved not unwilling to recognize West Saxon overlordship, providing it offered effective defence against the more backward Norwegian or Norwegian/Irish movements from the west and north. In return, the Saxon dynasty showed itself ready to respect the laws and customs of the new settlers. The initial basic division – useful, if simplified – between Christian English and heathen Dane broke down in the first half of the tenth century as missionaries became more active, and agrarian settlers found it expedient to accept the more sophisticated, literate religion of the community into which they had intruded themselves. Alfred's son Edward the Elder and Aethelflaed vigorously extended the burghal policy to Mercian lands. *Burhs* were built at strategic places such as Maldon, Witham, Bridgnorth, Tamworth, Eddisbury, Warwick and Buckingham. As the Danish armies submitted, their own fortifications were taken over at a great range of territory from Derby to Huntingdon, Cambridge, Northampton and Colchester. A special effort was made at Towcester, where the *burh* was provided with a stone wall. It was probably at this time that the effective shiring of the West Midlands took place, with territories roughly uniform in size and hidage, dependent on the fortified *burhs* of Gloucester, Worcester, Oxford, Warwick, Shrewsbury and Chester. Aethelflaed, Lady of the Mercians, died in 918, but Edward had little difficulty in taking over Mercia completely and, in a series of campaigns, forcing the submission of the Danish settlers still organized in their armies. By the time of his death all England south of the Humber was under his control.

Edward's son and successor, Athelstan, had been brought up at the Mercian court, and from this time serious danger of a political split between Wessex and Mercia ceased to exist, even though legal distinctions between the law of Wessex and that of Mercia continued to be drawn well into the twelfth century. Athelstan was a resolute warrior and great law-giver who deliberately built up the majesty and prestige of his kingship. He extended his authority to the north, and at Eamont near Penrith on 12 July 927 the kings of Scotland and Strathclyde, and the English lord of Bamburgh swore oaths of loyalty to him. He took possession of York and exacted tribute and formal oaths of loyalty from the leading Welsh princes at Hereford. He founded the see of St Germans for the Cornish people. Great councils were held, attended by Welsh princes as well as a multitude of ealdormen, bishops and thegns. There was a cosmopolitan aspect to his reign. Coins were struck with the inscription *rex totius Britanniæ*, king of all Britain. Exotic titles and language were used in his charters. Marriage arrangements with the ruling dynasties of France and Germany indicated his range and prestige: Hugh, duke of the Franks, married Eadhild, Athelstan's sister; another sister, Edith, married Otto I of Germany, and although she died in 946, long before her husband's imperial coronation at Rome, the German connection remained strong, particularly in cultural affairs. Athelstan brought up Harald Fair-hair's youngest son, Haakon, at his court, and was well known as a formidable figure in northern saga. Towards the end of his reign he inflicted a massive defeat at the battle of *Brunanburh* on a confede-ration of his enemies, Scottish, Hiberno-Norse and Scandinavian rulers. A long poem in praise of the victory was inserted in the Anglo-Saxon Chronicle, and Athelstan was honoured for making a greater slaughter of a host than had ever been made 'since the Angles and Saxons came hither from the east, invading Britain over the broad seas'.

Athelstan's political success in one important respect proved precocious. Northumbria had fallen into the hands of Scandinavian kings deeply involved in Irish affairs. Norwegians had settled in force in north-west England from the Wirral through the territory between Mersey and Ribble to Cumbria. The prospect of a long-lasting kingdom based on Dublin and York was by no means unthinkable and, though temporarily checked by Athelstan, was revived in the 940s. King Edmund, Athelstan's young brother (939–46), faced revived Norse power in York. The immediate results were curiously helpful. The powerful Danish group, still organized around their five main *burhs* in the Eastern Midlands (Leicester, Nottingham, Derby, Lincoln and Stamford), gladly submitted to him because they had previously been subjected by force under the Norsemen, 'for a long time in bonds of captivity to the heathen'.

Fear of the heathen on the part of the newly converted was a spur to the unification of Christian England. Edmund's death by assassination in 946 at the hands of a private enemy at the church of Pucklechurch in Gloucestershire was followed by an interim period under his brother Eadred (946–56) and a dangerous diarchy under his sons Edwy and Edgar (956–59), until the young Edgar emerged as sole ruler. The Scandinavians re-established themselves at York, but the defeat and death of Eric Bloodaxe, exiled son of the Norwegian king Harald Fairhair, in 954 brought to a symbolic end the first phase of Scandinavian attack and settlement in Britain. The Dublin/York axis, always fragile, was shattered, and full opportunity given for the integration of the greater part of historic Northumbria into the English kingdom.

King Eadred himself is a somewhat obscure and neglected figure. A young man, he was nevertheless clearly aware that he had not long to live. Unmarried, he made careful provision for his two nephews, Edmund's sons, to succeed him. The partition that resulted was unworkable, and it was probably only Edwy's early death that saved it from the test of civil war, or at least serious palace revolution. The mid-950s, however, saw elements of stability of great moment appearing in the political structure. It was either Eadred at the end of his life or the young Edwy who in 956 appointed young men to key positions, as ealdormen, from which they were to dominate English government in the succeeding generation: Aelfhere, ealdorman of Mercia, Aethelwold of East Anglia, and Byrhtnoth of Essex (who died heroically at the Battle of Maldon in 991); Aelfheah, Aelfhere's brother, was shortly afterwards appointed ealdorman of Hampshire. It was almost as if something of a vice-regal structure for the regions was already in the dynastic mind. Much of King Edgar's success (959–75) depended on his control of these great men, urged on as he clearly was by powerful clerical support. Edgar's legal code (Edgar IV), expressly issued for the improvement of public order and intended to be common to all 'who inhabit these islands', specifically mentioned the ealdormen who were to see to its dissemination – in this instance Aelfhere of Mercia, but also Oslac of Northumbria and Aethelwine of East Anglia.

Edgar's concern for public order shines through his surviving statements of law, which lay down regulations about the holding of courts in shires, hundreds and boroughs, and deal with basic ecclesiastical matters as well as secular, with fasts and feuds and payment of tithes, as well as theft and sureties and false judgments, with compensations and fair trading, as well as the price of wool or the systems of measurement as observed at Winchester. Edgar sensibly gave full recognition to the secular rights that were in force in the Danelaw, but where stolen goods or procedures for controlling theft were concerned he was adamant that all within his dominion, English, Danish or British, should observe the law. Politically and legally Edgar brought English kingship to new heights, and later generations looked back on his reign as a Golden Age.

The church gave full support and prospered in turn under the guidance of Archbishop Dunstan (960–88), Bishop Aethelwold of Winchester (963–84) and Oswald of Worcester (961–92), who also held York from 972. A great revival occurred in Benedictine monasticism, and powerful houses were set up or revived throughout the south and midlands, notably later deep into the East Midlands at Peterborough and Ramsey. These were closely linked with corresponding moves on the Continent, but served also as powerful forces moving towards a feeling of unity in England. Monks, well trained and literate, became active in the secular church. The *Regularis Concordia*, in 970 laid down general rules for Benedictine practice in England and gave a special place to the king and queen in the liturgy. Concentration on education in English as well as Latin helped to form common cultural ties; art and illumination of manuscripts flourished. Benefiting from a lull in Viking activity, the community enjoyed peace and prosperity. A massive and successful reform of the currency took place.

For reasons that may have had imperial undertones, Edgar was crowned with great solemnity at Bath in 973 when the king was thirty years of age. Shortly afterwards, a ceremony took place at Chester, when the king was rowed on a royal barge by kings and rulers drawn from the Celtic and Scandinavian worlds around Britain. There is a Roman and imperial flavour to the records that

71

have survived, some of them late, but the heart of the matter remains the strong kingship of the English now in process of creation. The northern version of the Chronicle caught the reality in its comment on Edgar's death, when it referred to him as the 'ruler of the English, friend of the West Saxons, protector of the Mercians'; and it reserved special praise for his defence of the country, so that there was 'no fleet so proud nor host so strong that it got itself prey in England as long as the noble king held the throne'. An occasional assertion of a superiority throughout all Britain was possible and helpful, but the substance of government, court systems, range of reformed coinage, and effective imposition of law rested within the narrower, but still impressive, bounds of a kingship of all England.

CHAPTER 4

The last century of Anglo-Saxon England

The last century of Anglo-Saxon England was a period of excep-
tional political turbulence. Dynastic uncertainty was one conspicuous feature. When Edgar died in 975 prospects seemed set fair for
the West Saxon house, but his young successor Edward the Martyr
was murdered at Corfe Castle in 978, and many believed that the
young king's stepmother had a hand in the plot in the interest of her
own son Ethelred. The reign of the unhappy Ethelred proved one of
the most disastrous in English history. Attacks from Scandinavia
were renewed in the 980s. The new raids tended to be more national
and political in nature than the movements of the earlier Viking
Age. They were often led by kings or princes, and their objectives
were loot, danegeld and, ultimately, political dominion. By the
second decade of the eleventh century English military force was so
demoralized and discredited that many welcomed the Danish king
Sweyn Forkbeard and his young son Cnut. Ethelred was exiled,
returned, but died in defeat in 1016. His son Edmund Ironside
fought bravely, and even succeeded at one stage in arranging a
temporary division of the kingdom, but he died before this division
could be effected, and Cnut was received as king of all England in
late 1016. He quickly accepted Christianity and proved in many
ways more English than the English. Even so, it should be remembered that the period from 1016 to the very end of 1066 saw no fewer
than four changes of dynasty in England. The victorious Cnut and
his sons governed the kingdom from 1016 to 1042, but the old
dynasty was then restored in the person of Edward the Confessor.
On his death in January 1066, the strongest man in the kingdom,
Harold Godwinson, Edward's own brother-in-law, was elected and
crowned Harold II of England. At Hastings a brief nine months later

Harold was killed, and victorious William the Norman succeeded to the English kingdom.

This dynastic uncertainty was mirrored by political uncertainty in another sense. Attempts to disrupt the unity of the kingdom of England proved abortive, but the boundaries of England were by no means fixed and inflexible. In the north there was a period of great fluctuation and change. Lothian, the land – some of it very fertile – in the south-east of modern Scotland from Edinburgh to Berwick, seems to have been granted by Edgar to the Scottish king Kenneth, probably in 973, and was finally confirmed as Scottish territory in the troubled days at the close of Ethelred's reign and in the early years of Cnut. To the north-west the lands that we now know as Cumbria, Cumberland and Westmorland, were in Scottish hands in the middle of the tenth century as part of the kingdom of Strathclyde, and this area remained disputed territory, mostly under Scottish lordship, until the last decade of the eleventh century. Not until the reign of William Rufus, when the Normans took possession of Carlisle in 1092, was the familiar boundary between England and Scotland foreshadowed, and then along a somewhat arbitrary division from Tweed to Solway that bore only incidental correlation with ancient frontiers, Roman or tribal. Indeed, the line as finally achieved in the course of the twelfth and thirteenth centuries cut right across two of the most potent political divisions of earlier days, the ancient English kingdom of Bernicia, and the British kingdom of Strathclyde.

There were no such dramatic fluctuations along the Welsh border. Offa's dyke remained the substantial line of division. Welsh pressure on Hereford remained a constant threat and erupted savagely during the middle of the eleventh century. Harold Godwinson made his reputation for political and military skill and ferocity precisely on this Hereford boundary in the years 1057–63. The family fortunes of the Godwins were closely tied up with the question of English control of the Wye and the Severn, and associated too with the rise of Bristol and the fostering of continuous trade along the Severn sea to Ireland, and above all to Dublin. Cornwall, meantime, in the course of the tenth century had been brought firmly and securely under West Saxon control.

There was a time when these dynastic upsets and the general political turbulence were taken as symptoms of a deep-rooted malaise in English affairs, a setback in the process of the making of a nation. Deeper investigation proved this view false. It is now universally recognized that by 1066 England was one of the best-developed monarchies and probably the wealthiest in Western Europe. The most clear-cut indication of this strength comes in the field of finance and government. It is sometimes wryly said that common taxation is the one certain test of nationhood, and on that score England was well on the way to becoming a nation by 1066. The system of taxation was basically simple but effective. The geld was a land tax that worked, and the compounds *danegeld* (payment to the Danes to desist from raiding) or *heregeld* (protection payment to an army or to a navy) merely signified variation in purpose, not in methods of assessing or collecting. Each estate in the country was assessed, normally in units known as hides or carucates, or sulungs in Kent, and paid according to a standard rate whenever a geld was levied. In the reign of Edward the Confessor geld appears to have been levied normally at a standard rate of two shillings a hide annually. William I's massive gelds, under which the community groaned, trebled that figure. Regional variation and complexities in methods of assessment, notably in East Anglia, should not obscure the basic fact that England was accustomed to a regular national system of taxation; experience had been bought the hard way, in buying off the Dane.

A remarkably successful currency underpinned the general financial expertise of the country. The only coin in regular use was the silver penny, but the standard was high, and the techniques of production and control a model for other communities. Scandinavians in particular borrowed heavily from English experience when they introduced their own native communities to regular coinage in the course of the eleventh century. Edgar's reform of the currency in 973 was based on a few simple but effective principles, based for the most part on English precedents. Central control was achieved by the issue of dies, at first from one central die-cutting agency. Profit came to the crown – for coinage was a regalian right of the first order – at the point when the moneyers from the localities received their dies. Coins were then struck at the local mint by these accredited moneyers. After a period of time – six years initially after the reform of 973, dropping to two or three years during the reign of the Confessor – the coinage was recalled, types were changed, and the local moneyers again went to the die-cutting centre to buy the dies from which the coins could be struck. They made their own profit at the local mints, paying a fixed sum, presumably in relation to output, to the local royal officer at a fixed time after their return with the new dies. Savage legal penalties imposed on false moneyers or moneyers who betrayed their trust helped to maintain the high standard of the currency. The name of the mint and the name of the moneyer normally appeared on the coin; degrees of artistic achievement varied, but at their best the late Anglo-Saxon pennies achieved a fine standard both aesthetically and economically, serving as essential instruments of exchange.

In its secretarial as well as in its financial aspects late Anglo-Saxon England showed some advanced features. There was no chancery by that name, and no officer that we know of for certain became chancellor until the time of the Norman Conquest, but there was an efficient writing office at the royal court. There was a long tradition of scribal activity around the court, expressed, for example, in the purely legal field by the framing of the law codes so characteristic of the rulers of late Anglo-Saxon England. Evidence of Ethelred's achievements in this field exist in the survival of many codes or partial codes issued during his reign. The finest product of all, the laws of Cnut, were still regarded as an authoritative guide to legal custom in England a century later, long after the Norman Conquest. In matters concerning the transmission of land, too, there was great tradition and experience. Land charters survive in great numbers from the last century of Anglo-Saxon England as evidence of legitimacy of title to ownership of land. The chance of survival throws natural emphasis on the ecclesiastical element in the solemn land charter. Churches alone were capable of providing safety and security in which an archive could be kept, and some religious houses proved very faithful guardians of their title deeds. For example, as late as the fourteenth century a conscientious monk of Winchester was able to copy out a whole series of solemn Anglo-

Saxon landbooks, charters of which otherwise we would have no or very little trace. Exact work in diplomatic studies has shown us that often the local beneficiaries drew up the charter as it now exists, but the standardization in general format, the witness lists, and the tone and purpose of the documents remind us again that we are dealing with a, for the most part, national phenomenon. It was natural that a land charter should be authorized by the king in solemn council at the *witenagemot*, the assembly of wise men, even if it was drawn up by the beneficiary. Our charters record either royal gifts of land, immunity and rights, or a transfer of land immunity and rights secular or ecclesiastical, sanctioned by the king and approved in his council.

More important in many respects than the charter was the other conspicuous product of the secretarial side of government, the sealed writ. This has been described as the most important English contribution to the art of government in the early Middle Ages, and is undoubtedly an indicator of the relatively advanced nature of Anglo-Saxon institutional life. Charters were ponderous documents, heavy, Latin (though with the bounds of estates in English), meant to act as permanent evidence and a permanent record of transactions. Writs were different – for the most part in Anglo-Saxon, brief, direct government orders addressed to the men in the localities capable of carrying out the orders. King Edward the Confessor, for example, when he wanted to make sure that the priests at St Paul's Minster were exercising their rights of jurisdiction adequately and that their domestic economy was in order, issued the following writ, which was to be read aloud to all the people gathered together in the shire courts in which St Paul's was known to have interest:

> King Edward sends friendly greetings to my bishops and my earls and all my thegns in the shires in which my priests in Paul's Minster have land. And I inform you that it is my will that they be entitled to their sake and their soke [jurisdiction] both within borough and without, and entitled now to as good laws – as fully and as completely – as ever they were in all things in the days of any king or of any bishop. And I forbid them to receive into their

Minster any more priests than their estates can bear and they themselves desire. And I will not permit anyone to do them any wrong in any matter.

It would be a simplification to say that the writ or the writ-charter replaced the solemn charter in the last stages of Anglo-Saxon administration. Writ and charter should be seen as complementary, the one more immediate, the other more permanent. But undoubtedly, possession of a copy of a writ referring to the transmission of land or of rights was held to give as good title as a charter and was treated as such in Domesday Book. The use of a seal to authenticate the written word attached to a writ represents an advance in sophistication in the art of government. This custom became widespread in the eleventh century, and the survival of dies at Westminster and at other great ecclesiastical institutions indicates the general nature of their use. Eleventh-century elaboration at the royal level, possibly based on German imperial models, helped to build up the complete fabric of the perfected royal writ. In essence it was and remained a royal letter, and its use was by no means confined to transactions relating to land, although naturally most of the surviving examples deal with this commodity, with its inherent attributes of permanence. Indeed, the writ-mandate in many respects must have been more significant than the writ-charter. It was a means of articulating government, of keeping the king and his councillors in close touch with the localities – a vital element in the creation of a nation.

It is sometimes said that the history of government in Anglo-Saxon England is the history of local government, and in a limited sense that is true. For most of the inhabitants of England, contact with royal government was fleeting and short. The realities of government rested in the lord's hall, the hundred court, and, rarely, on the great formal occasions, the shire court. In no field is this more true than the purely judicial. There was in a sense a hierarchy of courts, but not according to the fully formulated late medieval pattern of established judiciaries linked from central courts, with justices on eyre or at assizes. Ultimate judicial authority undoubtedly rested with the royal court. The king's function was to give judgment, and an element of this personal authority persisted throughout the Middle Ages. The king was surrounded at his court by his councillors, and at set times, associated normally with the great ecclesiastical feasts, it was customary for the king to deliberate with his council and give opinion in a *witenagemot*. In moments of great crisis – succession to the throne, or a king's minority – this assembly, the great council, took on a special authority of its own, though it was not in any intelligible wider sense of the term a constitutional check on the monarchy. Great judicial causes, disputes between leading and national figures, quarrels over policy, matters concerning provision to an earldom, would normally be settled in the *witan*. For ordinary routine business, however, we look lower in the hierarchy. In this respect we need to remember that one of the great achievements of the period, for which full credit is not always given, is the establishment of a pattern of local government that was to survive in essence fully recognizable throughout the medieval period and well into the modern world. The shire court and the hundred court provide the most enduring testimonial, short of the monarchy itself, to positive Anglo-Saxon success in the art of government.

The shiring of England, that is the dividing of England into, for the most part, manageable units of local administration for military, fiscal and judicial purposes, was a product of the period between the reign of Alfred and the Norman Conquest. The shire was basically a West Saxon institution, associated in Wessex itself sometimes with ancient kingdoms such as Kent, sometimes with units of territorial administration dependent on royal townships, such as Somerset with its township of Somerton, Dorset with its township of Dorchester, or Wiltshire with its township of Wilton. The maintenance of the integrity of Western Mercia nevertheless involved the extension of this shiring system to areas such as Warwickshire and Shropshire, although the process was not complete until the early eleventh century, when, for example, an earlier Winchcombeshire was absorbed into the larger stretch of Gloucestershire, probably because of the special naval and military demands of the Severn estuary. Extension of Christian English authority further east led to further elaboration of the shire system. Danish armies in the early tenth century had grouped themselves into territorial units focused on their fortified *burhs*, and much of the whole complex organization of the Danelaw south of the Humber was already known by 942 as the 'territory of the five *burhs*', that is to say the land dependent on Lincoln, Nottingham, Leicester, Derby and Stamford. These *burhs* with the exception of Stamford, became the chief administrative centres of the new shires. Stamford was in a special position because of the compelling needs of naval defence of the long and vulnerable coastline between the Humber and Wash, and the concentration of authority on the great base of Lincoln ensured the establishment of the huge shire of Lincolnshire, with consequent downgrading of Stamford in the administrative hierarchy. A similar military compulsion also applied further north when it came to the shiring of the community, and the territory dependent on York and to the east of the Pennines provided the nucleus of what became the largest of all English shires: Yorkshire. Subdivisions known as trithings or ridings came to ease the administrative difficulties consequent on shire size in both Yorkshire and Lincolnshire. Elsewhere in England the divisions were also reasonably clearly defined. East Anglia fell apart naturally into its two ancient divisions of Suffolk and Norfolk. To the north-west the complexity of a turbulent border brought some obscurities. In Domesday Book there was no Lancashire, merely the territory between the Ribble and the Mersey; it was the new feudal regularization of the border that brought into being our familiar modern shape of Lancashire, Westmorland and Cumberland in north-west England. In the north-east Durham and Northumberland emerged only very slowly, and then under feudal compulsion; the turbulence of the border in this area also made special arrangements necessary. But the shiring of England was largely complete by the reign of Edward the Confessor – indeed, substantially by the reign of Cnut.

There is one major complication to the general story of the shiring of England. Under Alfred the ideal arrangement had undoubtedly been to establish in each shire a responsible nobleman, known as an ealdorman, with full authority to look after the royal interests in the shire. Under pressure of events, notably military events, and as the range of English kingship grew greater, this arrangement no longer proved satisfactory. Key appointments in the 950s, as we have seen, heralded the appearance of men, still termed ealdormen, whose authority extended over more than one shire. The process reached its climax under Cnut. The Danish king (as he was after 1019) governed an empire, not merely a kingdom, and needed trusted men to look after royal interests over large regions. The result was an emergence of a new class of men, known now under the Danish name of earl rather than ealdorman, who took over what were virtually vice-regal functions, usually in territories corresponding to the ancient kingdoms, but also at times – a complicating and neglected fact – in one or more of the newer shires. By the middle of the eleventh century three families had emerged with a generation and more of this sort of experience behind them, as men of recognized earlish rank. In Wessex Godwin, the son of a Sussex thegn, had proved a most loyal supporter of ·Cnut. Married to a Danish princess, Gytha, he sired a large family, the ablest of whom, Harold II of England and Tostig, earl of Northumbria (1055–65), were killed in the great battles of 1066, together with their younger brothers Leofwine and Gyrth. The second of the families of eleventh-century earls was that of Leofric of Mercia. His widow Godiva was still alive in 1067, and her grandsons Edwin and Morcar played a prominent part in the events of 1066 and in the uneasy post-Conquest situation in England. Siward, earl of Northumbria, was the third heroic figure to found a family of earls, and it was his son Waltheof, married to the Conqueror's niece, whose political execution in 1076 was held by many to mark the decisive end of the old order. All these men, the earls of the second quarter of the eleventh century, operated at a political level different from the old routine ealdorman's business of the shire court. The ealdormen were steadily replaced by earls and other royal officers, notably the shire reeves, or sheriffs, until the term ealdormen itself came somewhat incongruously to survive only in the sense of the worthy, dignified aldermen of towns.

The earls, for all their political power, did not necessarily in themselves indicate grave disruptive weakness in the structure of the English monarchy. It is true that they showed tendencies to develop into a small and exclusive class, but these tendencies were never fully realized or exploited. Rivalries between the families, and between individual male members of mature age within the same family, kept a rough balance. Certainly, by the 1050s it was expected that the Godwin family would succeed to the earldom of Wessex and the family of Leofric to that of Mercia, but the rights of the king and the *witan* were exercised at every appointment, as far as we can judge. The office of earl remained an office, subject to appointment by king and *witan*, and capable of being withdrawn either by the king or through pressure from beneath. It was such royal favour that led Tostig, a representative of Godwin's house, to be appointed to the earldom of Northumbria in 1055, and it was pressure from below – that is, rejection by the influential thegns of the province – that led to his removal in 1065, an event that folded politically into the precipitation of the Norman Conquest itself.

Some interest lies in a comparison and contrast with events in Normandy at the same time. There, in the 1050s and early 1060s, the ducal family, and notably William himself, were gathering around them a formidable group of warriors, who were to make their fortunes by the side of their leader in succeeding generations. These men were feudal subordinates, tied to their lords by the most rigid feudal bonds. English earls represented a very different type of man, their authority public and official to a degree unthinkable in the Norman duchy. The contrast between Leofwine Godwinson and William FitzOsbern, or Aelfgar, son of Leofric, and Hugh Lupus, earl of Chester, provides a vital clue to the contrast in social structure between territorial England and feudal Normandy.

Within the earldoms the shires continued to exercise an independent existence. The shire court was normally held twice a year, at Easter and at Michaelmas, and was presided over by the earl and the bishop or their deputies, and increasingly, one suspects, by the chief of the royal reeves. Its business had much to do with finance and with geld, and with the administration of justice, but it still remained a court where important causes could be heard, and one that could be afforced by men from other shires where need arose. The shire court was also a great social occasion, when the chief men in the shire assembled and when all the unrecorded detail covering the political business of the shire, the sending and provisioning of contingents to the *fyrd*, and practical matters concerning the well-being of all inhabitants of the shire, were discussed. It was also an ecclesiastical occasion, often overlapping in timing into an episcopal synod.

The institutional identity and continuity of the shire is a fact of great importance in English social history. Routine business could not normally be attended to at the shire court, and responsibility for this fell increasingly on the smaller territorial units, the hundreds, or *wapentakes* as they were known over much of the Danelaw. From the time of Edward the Elder these seem to have been the essential peace-keeping agencies over most of the country. Under Edgar they were regularized, and it was laid down that hundred courts should be held every four weeks. Under Cnut it was said expressly that no appeal could be made to the king unless justice had first been sought in the hundred court. Increasingly, hundreds tended to fall into private hands in late Anglo-Saxon England. This brings us face to face with one of the puzzles that surround the growth of the feudal order. In parts of the Continent private jurisdiction reached such a point that the public courts fell into decay. The English situation was very different. We experience in England the same growth of secular lordship as elsewhere, but private jurisdiction was more restricted. Any great landowner and any great ecclesiastical house would possess rights of jurisdiction over their own tenants and would also possess territorial rights, which were sometimes referred to as sokes. Such rights were implicit in the grant of any charter or landbook and were customarily expressed in the last century of Anglo-Saxon England by means of terms such as sake and soke. The great landowners, we must remember, were also invariably slave-owners, and jurisdiction over the slaves was virtually limitless. But over freemen, sake and soke and associated rights were the result of a franchise expressly granted ultimately by the king. In the last resort, the right to hold a court at which freemen were suitors was a delegated right from the monarch himself.

There remains one important institution in the life of the community about which we have said little: the church. The church was involved in all the workings of society in this Carolingian theocratic world. There was a time when, partly because of the bad reputation of Stigand, the last Anglo-Saxon archbishop of Canterbury, and partly because of fresh comparisons with the Anglo-Norman world, the reputation of the late Anglo-Saxon church stood low. This is no longer so. The Benedictine revival of the mid-tenth century is now properly read as one of the most impressive religious revivals in early European history. St Dunstan and his helpers revitalized the church in England, and not only in its monastic aspects. A literary renaissance in the vernacular took place in the late tenth and early eleventh centuries, with Aelfric and Wulfstan of Worcester and York as the two principal figures. The appointment of trained monks of the reformed Benedictine order to the episcopate brought a high standard to office – so much so that the reinforced attack threatened by heathen Scandinavians resulted ultimately in the conversion of Scandinavia itself. Cnut's high reputation as a Christian king, a supporter of the church and a visitor to Rome, owes much to men of the stamp of Wulfstan, trained in the new vigorous ideals of the reform church. It is true that the church remained somewhat old-fashioned by the side of the Continental reformers of the mid-eleventh century. Celibacy was not enforced among the lower clergy; pluralism, or apparent pluralism, was not uncommon; and by up-to-date standards many of the leading figures in the English church in the reign of the Confessor were to some measure guilty of simony. Nevertheless, in essentials there is much to be said for the view that the old English church was by no means as backward as its detractors, notably its Norman detractors, made out.

If we take, therefore, our stand in the 1060s, we can see England as a tempting prize indeed for a conqueror. It was wealthy, accustomed to government, and capable of producing leaders of the calibre of Harold Godwinson in the military field, and of the calibre of an Ealdred of York or Wulfstan II (St Wulfstan) of Worcester in the ecclesiastical sphere. The substructure of the English nation was secure and well formed. It was left now to new Norman masters to force it into characteristic Norman moulds.

CHAPTER 5

The Norman Conquest:
the reigns of the Norman kings

The trials of the Danish wars, the triumphs of Edgar and the reformed church, and the subsequent seesaw of political dominance between Anglo-Saxons and Danes had welded the English kingdom into a unit. Firm direction was now needed if such unity were to be maintained and the proper balance between economic resources and institutional life established. The Danish Cnut had pointed the way to one possible solution, but his delegation of virtual vice-regal powers to great earls was sensible only when England was taken as part of a greater Scandinavian complex, and some elements in the reign of Edward the Confessor must be read as symptoms of the failure of such a scheme. The Normans had different and, ultimately, highly successful solutions to the English problem.

Norman involvement in English affairs began early in the eleventh century, when Ethelred in 1002, as part of his general plan for safeguarding his southern shores against Scandinavian pressures, married Emma, daughter of Duke Richard II of Normandy. The Norman duchy itself, established on the ruin of the ancient county of Rouen as the Danelaw of France in 911, was entering a prosperous expansionist phase, which, despite a turbulent period of civil war in the late 1030s and early 1040s, was to result in the creation of the most powerful feudal unit in France. During much of this period of growth, to the time of her death in 1051, Emma remained a powerful influence in English affairs. Her sons by the English king Ethelred, Edward the Confessor and Alfred, fled to Normandy in the days of their father's defeat. She herself married his conqueror Cnut, by whom she had another son, Harthacnut. When Edward the Confessor ultimately succeeded in 1042 he was constrained to curb the influence and authority of his Norman mother, the Lady of

Winchester. Edward was by no means the wholesale Normanizer of some historical legend, but he continued to keep close contact with Normandy, his home during critical formative years of exile from 1014 to 1042. He relied on some key Norman and French figures in the church; prominent among their number were Robert of Jumièges, archbishop of Canterbury until forced into exile in 1052; William, bishop of London (1051–75); and the king's physician, Baldwin, abbot of Bury St Edmunds (1062–97). In secular affairs he had also Norman advisers, not all of them particularly effective, but helping to give something of a counterbalance to the rapidly increasing authority of Earl Godwin and his sons. At some stage, possibly in 1051–2 during the peak period of disgrace of the Godwins, Edward made an approach to his young kinsman William, duke of Normandy, Edward's mother's grand-nephew, to keep the possibility of election to the English throne open to him. In Norman eyes this was later held to be a firm promise of the right to succeed, a promise which it was not in fact in Edward's power to give. The presence of a powerful (and increasingly powerful) duke with interest, no matter how amorphous, to the succession in England, cannot have been altogether disadvantageous to Edward as the military and political authority of Harold Godwinson and his brothers reached its climax in the late 1050s and 1060s. Harold's curious and surely ambiguous embassy to the Norman court, recorded in detail in the Bayeux Tapestry, may well have been calculated by Edward as a means of keeping the succession dubious.

In 1066 all doubt was resolved in war. Harold succeeded in early January to reign for nine months, 'uneasily', as a chronicler put it. Scandinavian ambitions were destroyed in September by Harold's great victory at Stamford Bridge, when the Norwegian king Harald Hardrada and the English Harold's disaffected brother Tostig, former earl of Northumbria, were both killed. On 14 October at Battle, some seven miles from Hastings, William won a savagely hard-fought victory, and so, as his eulogist William of Poitiers expressed it, won England in a single battle. The eulogist exaggerated. It was a full six years before the Normans could feel thoroughly safe in England from English rebellion and from Scandinavian pressure. Even in the last years of the Conqueror's reign, fear of

Danish invasion prompted William to bring over what the Chronicler termed 'a greater force of Frenchmen than he had ever seen before'. Yet in his exaggeration William of Poitiers also foresaw the truth. The victory at Hastings ensured a conquest that was to be enduring and, indeed, permanent in its effects.

For eighty-eight years after 1066 there was a Norman king on the throne of England. William I (1066–87) was succeeded by two of his sons in turn, William II (1087–1100) and Henry I (1100–35). His grandson Stephen, son of his daughter Adela, held the crown from 1135 to 1154, after a disputed succession and a period of civil war which at times and in some regions degenerated into near anarchy. For much of this period Normandy was also governed by the English king, and the complicated political pattern cannot be disentangled unless the consequences of the double tie are recognized. Under the terms of the Conqueror's will, his eldest son Robert, proud, brave and incompetent, succeeded to the duchy, and much Anglo-Norman effort and energy over the succeeding nineteen years went in the undoing of this settlement. William himself on his deathbed is said to have prophesied misfortune to come because of Robert's stupidity. William II took the duchy under his protection in pawn when his eldest brother went on crusade (1097–1100), and the cold, calculating Henry I virtually conquered the duchy at the battle of Tinchebrai in 1106. Robert was kept in prison until his death in 1133, and his son William Clito, used as a political pawn by the French king for most of his life, died after an unsuccessful attempt to assume the authority of count in Flanders in 1127.

The disputed succession of 1135 brought the Norman question back into the open. Henry I had struggled after the death of his own son William in 1120 to ensure a peaceful succession for his daughter Matilda. The barons pledged support reluctantly, and their reluctance grew after Matilda's marriage in 1128 to Geoffrey Plantagenet, count of Anjou, regarded as a rival or worse by many Normans. The birth of Prince Henry, the future Henry II, in 1133 might have eased matters, but Matilda's personal unpopularity told against her, and Stephen's decisive moves on the death of the old king brought him immediate political support and success. A slow rally to Matilda and consequent civil war gave Geoffrey and the Angevins their opportunity. Matilda's cause was unsuccessful in England, but by 1144 Normandy was in her husband's hands. Very sensibly, he had his son, the young Henry, recognized as duke of Normandy in 1150. On Geoffrey's death in 1151, Henry succeeded also to Anjou. It was not the least of the forces that made for his recognition as Stephen's heir to England in 1153 that so many of the great Anglo-Norman aristocratic families clamoured for a reunification of duchy and kingdom.

The Norman contribution to the making of the English nation was complex, elaborate and deep-rooted; certain features of it emerge clear and direct. The great historian William of Malmesbury, writing in the 1120s, found a perfect phrase to sum up Norman achievements when he declared that 'they plunder their subjects, though they protect them from others.' He modified his attitude to this plunder by stressing their generosity in religious matters so that you could see churches rise in every village and monasteries, built after a style never seen before, in the towns and cities. But in his insistence on their ability to protect their subjects he touched the heart of the matter. The twin pillars of their military success – the building of castles and the use of skilled cavalrymen – proved also to be the firm supports of their governmental activities. Contemporaries attributed their immediate success to the use of *munitiones*, castles, which, it was claimed, had hitherto been unknown in England. This was not strictly true, as Norman favourites had started the practice in the reign of the Confessor, certainly in the Western Marches at Hereford, Richard's Castle and Ewyas Harold; but this was fringe activity, important in potential rather than substance. It was the Norman Conquest that brought the need for castle-building, calculated to overawe as well as to supply safe headquarters for government. The Tower of London and the surviving portion of Colchester Castle still stand today as witness to Norman enterprise. William's campaign to the north in 1170–1 was accompanied by a spate of castle-building at strategic points, notably at York, Chester and Stafford. Some great tenants-in-chief also built on a substantial scale: William FitzOsbern in the early years of the Conquest (he died in 1071) set up the great hall of his castle at Chepstow, a key strategic site.

13 Bury St Edmunds artist's view in the twelfth century of Danish armies
landing in England, *c*.869.

18 A scene from Aelfric's Old Testament, showing the king and the *witan* as a judicial court, imposing the death penalty.

ᵹeþ cƿam ᵹeᵹaꝼum phaꝩao mæꞇꞇe pæꞇh

14–16   Silver pennies of Offa (*centre*),
Alfred and Ethelred (Exeter mint,
probably *c.*997–1003).

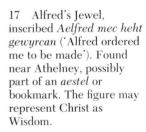

17   Alfred's Jewel,
inscribed *Aelfred mec heht
gewyrcan* ('Alfred ordered
me to be made'). Found
near Athelney, possibly
part of an *aestel* or
bookmark. The figure may
represent Christ as
Wisdom.

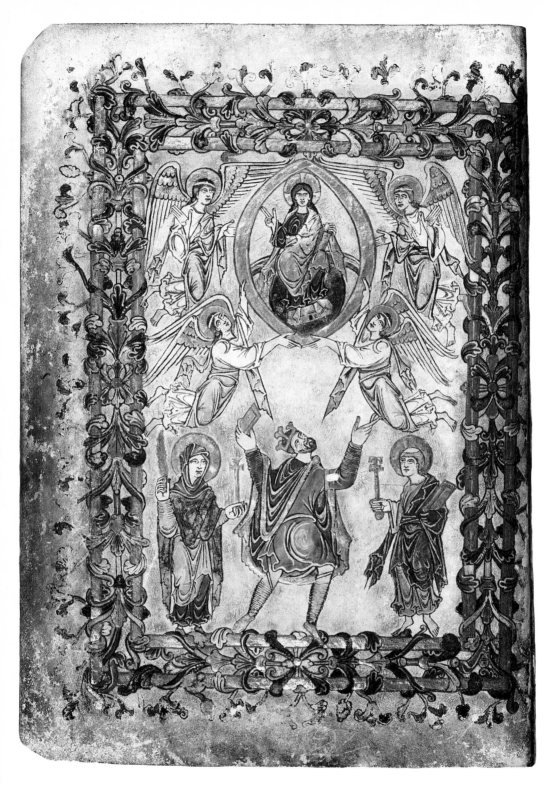

19   Frontispiece of the New Minster Charter, Winchester, in which King
Edgar, between the Virgin Mary and St Peter, offers the charter to Christ.
20   St Dunstan at the feet of Christ. The inscription above the saint's figure
may be in Dunstan's own hand.

Dunstanum memet clemens rogo xpe tuere
tenarias me non sina sorbsisse procellas:

PRINCIPIUM IANR̄ SANCIT TROPEC CAPRICORNUS
IANUARIUS HABET DIES XXXI LUNA ...
III AAAA PIANIURE KALENDARUM QĒS CONCIDITUR AGNUS.
B B IIII N Isidorus ponī gaudet in ordine quadris.

21   Ploughing in January: from an eleventh-century astronomical treatise.

23   Hunting scene from an eleventh-century calendar.

SEPTEMBER HABET
XVI   H F
RT SEP
PRISCO
DIES

22   Haymaking in June: from an illuminated manuscript.

24   Harold in majesty after his coronation, formally but falsely crowned, according to Norman sentiment. Bayeux Tapestry.

25   Harold in the months after coronation: note the twisted figure of the king, the comet in the upper margin indicating trouble, and the ghost ships in the lower margin, the quarter from which retribution would come. Bayeux Tapestry.

By the end of William I's reign communications along all the main roads and in most of the bigger urban centres were safeguarded by the presence of significant and often substantial stone castles.

Of equal social importance was the host of smaller fortifications, for the most part the familiar pudding-basin mottes with their attached baileys, which sprang up as the feudal settlement proved enduring. The origins of the motte are still a matter of some obscurity, but there is no doubting their proliferation in the mid-eleventh century, and it may well be that Norman experience in England confirmed the motte as the most effective means of imposing dominical authority on an agrarian neighbourhood and of providing local military lords with a seemly, efficient and distinctive home base. At least 700 mottes and perhaps another 250 or so ringworks with their strong gatehouses and fortified inner structures were put up in England and Wales, mostly in the century and a half after the Conquest. They were widespread through the country, with a naturally heavy concentration along the Welsh border, and can be still enjoyed as part of the landscape in places as divergent as Rayleigh in Essex, Bronllys and Tretower in Breconshire, Launceston in Cornwall, or the inner heart of Cardiff castle. Even within huge later castles, such as Arundel or Windsor, the primitive early Norman motte can often be seen. From them, the local lords, tenants-in-chief or subtenants could deploy their posses of knights to maintain local peace. From them the local lords could exercise authority, legitimately if held in check by the king, the royal officers, the church and the local courts, illegally and tyranically if the bonds of superior lordship were loosened.

For if castles were the major and most conspicuous addition to the English landscape attributable to the Normans, the presence and nature of the men who manned them should never be ignored. Knights on horseback were new to England in 1066. Cavalry training itself was, as always, long and arduous, and initially very much the preserve of the newcomers, experienced in Continental warfare. Their control of specialist functions and their expected reward in the shape of fiefs on great estates set them apart from the subject English people, and it was only slowly that the barriers were broken down. Not that these barriers were in the strict sense racial. It was William of Malmesbury again who told us that the Normans, for all their faults, their violence and treachery, were the most polite of people; and that they intermarried with their subjects. Nevertheless, their skill as mounted soldiers and their use of castles undoubtedly set them apart and gave them social as well as military control of their new kingdom. They were not great legal innovators, but on one matter they were firm in a most revealing manner, and that was in the institution of the so-called *murdrum* fine. If a Frenchman were killed (or a body found that could not be proved to be English), a heavy fine was laid on the hundred, the territorial neighbourhood. This imposition of a corporate penalty is one of the best symptoms we have of the elements of force behind the claims to legitimate lordship. The *murdrum* fine echoes the cry of occupying forces throughout the ages.

There is one further general element in the Norman settlement that demands attention. Hunting preserves were known before the Conquest, but it was left to the Normans to introduce the concept of a forest, that is to say, of land kept for hunting purposes placed outside the workings of a normal law of the land. As a twelfth-century commentator put it elegantly and accurately, the laws of the forest came not from the common law of the realm but from the will of princes; so that what was done in accordance with them was said not to be just absolutely, but just according to forest law. The creation of the New Forest in Hampshire made immediate savage impact. It appears that William I found some 75,000 acres of almost deserted country, added to it a further 15–20,000 acres of inhabited land and evicted some 500 families as a safeguard against poaching. With later additions of a further 10–20,000 acres, the New Forest remained a potent example of forest policy, but it was only one among many great forest tracts. At one stage the whole of Essex was subject to forest law under Henry I, and at its height in the early thirteenth century, forests were to be found in no fewer than thirty-three of the thirty-nine shires into which England was divided. Forest law became the symbol of the harsh and cruel side of royal government. In the early stages mutilation was the accepted penalty for poaching offences. The Anglo-Saxon Chronicler com-

Castles built by William I
or with his sanction

Odo of Bayeux The names of some prominent tenants, placed near some important sources of their territorial wealth

Main roads

0 20 40 60 80 100
Miles

Carlisle

Newcastle

Durham

Alan of Brittany

Robert of Mortain
Hugh d'Avranches

William of Percy

Stamford Bridge

Archbishop of York

York

Bishop of Durham

Ilbert de Lacy

Roger of Poitou

William of Warenne

Gilbert de Gand

Roger of Poitou

Roger de Busli

William of Percy

Rhuddlan
Robert of Rhuddlan

Chester

Lincoln

Odo of Bayeux

GWYNEDD

Hugh d'Avranches

Robert of Stafford

Henry de Ferrers

Nottingham

Alan of Brittany

William Peverel

Stafford

Derby

Roger de Tosni

Ivo Taillebois

POWYS

Lichfield

Shrewsbury

Roger of Montgomery

Hugh of Grandmesnil

Leicester

Peterborough

Ely

Norwich

Roger Bigod

Thorkill of Arden

Count of Meulan

Countess Judith

Robert Malet

Odo of Bayeux

Urse d'Abitot

Coventry

Warwick

Huntingdon

Bury St Edmunds

Richard of Clare

Ipswich

Worcester

Northampton

Cambridge

DEHEUBARTH

Hereford

Brecon

Roger de Lacy

William FitzOsbern
died 1071

Gloucester

Bedford

Buckingham

Aubrey de Vere

Robert d'Oilly

Hertford

Colchester

Geoffrey of Mandeville

Suen of Essex

Berkhamsted

Eustace of Boulogne

Chepstow

Pembroke

Roger d'Ivry

Oxford

Abingdon

St Albans

London

Rochester

Cardiff

Bristol

Bath

Malmesbury

Wallingford

Westminster

Windsor

Canterbury

Lanfranc

Geoffrey Bishop of Coutances

Edward of Salisbury

Guildford

Odo of Bayeux

Richard of Clare

Hugh of Montfort

Dover

Wells

Old Sarum

Winchester

William of Braose

Robert of Mortain

Baldwin the Sheriff

Hugh de Port

Southampton

Chichester

Bramber

Lewes

Hastings

Robert of Eu

Exeter

Corfe

Dorchester

Arundel

Pevensey

William of Warenne

Judhael of Totnes

Roger of Montgomery

Robert of Mortain

Totnes

ENGLAND DURING THE REIGN OF WILLIAM THE CONQUEROR

plained bitterly that William I loved the stags as if he were their father, and his Norman and Angevin successors were tenacious of their forest rights, which brought them great financial gain as well as social pleasure. In Magna Carta itself and throughout the constitutional struggles of the thirteenth century, opposition to arbitrary royal government was directed sharply against the law of the forest.

There was, however, another side to royal government, operating not so much on an arbitrary basis but with proper respect to law and custom. Within the limits of the age, the Normans perfected the instruments of executive government. They also introduced an aristocracy that was new both in personnel and, to a large measure, in principle. By and large the Normans were neither great theoreticians nor great innovators. They were pragmatic men, whose special gifts enabled them to revivify old institutions and make them work. There is no substantial legislative programme to look back to as a product of Norman government. In local affairs the old divisions of shire, hundred and *wapentake* were virtually unchanged. The Normans were men who by nature sought to make the traditional efficient. They governed England at a time of general economic revival throughout Western Europe, and too much credit for greater wealth and prosperity, and the general glitter, should not go exclusively in the direction of these somewhat harsh masters of the feudal world. Yet there are achievements in the fields of executive government and of the implantation of a new aristocratic principle that are great enough to merit special attention.

We have already seen how the summoning of a great council of the realm was a feature of Anglo-Saxon institutional life. Under William and his successors these *witans* were held more regularly, in theory at least at Christmas, Easter and Whitsun, and were more systematized and, indeed, urbanized, so that Gloucester, Winchester and Westminster became the accepted normal places of meeting. All the chief landowners, lay and ecclesiastical, were expected to attend or to explain why they could not do so; and these great councils became under the Conqueror important political assemblies, at which decisions concerning peace or war, or the setting in train of such vital administrative measures as the survey leading to Domesday Book could be made widely known. The early Norman kings were all, in their different ways, masters at controlling these councils. The first William did so in a dignified manner, the second with a great deal of bluster, while Henry I used a combination of guile, cunning and fear. Stephen failed to do so, and much of the political trouble of his reign resulted from the failure.

The best example of the great council at work comes from the record of events that led to the creation of Domesday Book. At Christmas 1085 a council was held at Gloucester, where King William, after deep discussion with his counsellors, magnates, bishops and abbots, initiated the elaborate procedures needed to launch a gigantic survey of the wealth of the newly conquered kingdom. The whole administration was quickly involved. Sheriffs must have been alerted from the outset, collecting written evidence on tenure and tax capacity, and seeing to it that urban records were also ready for use. The kingdom was divided into seven regions, and commissioners were appointed from among the great men not interested personally in the region in question to check on the results of the investigation. Over the whole country the shire courts became the institutions at which the information was moulded into manageable shape. The survey itself, conducted on a manorial base within each shire, systematically recorded basic facts: the name of the manor, who held it now and who had held it in the past, its arable capacity, the amount of geld or tax exacted from it, the nature of the peasant population, ancillary sources of wealth, such as woodland, mills and fisheries, the total value of the estate and, in some instances, whether or not more could be taken from it. It is likely that the survey was completed in the months between the Christmas council of 1085–6 and the late summer of 1086. The oath of Salisbury, which King William exacted from all land-holding men of any account in early August, was almost certainly associated with the construction of Domesday Book, and it seems likely that the sophisticated first volume was completed before the death of the Conqueror in September 1087.

One must not exaggerate; there were slips and omissions, occasional errors and duplications. The eastern counties of Essex, Suffolk and Norfolk were never brought into final form and remain in the volume known as Domesday Book, volume II, as an unfinished but very full product of the survey. Domesday Book, volume I, covers the rest of the kingdom, apart from areas of the north outside the shire system, and is a bureaucratic triumph, a miracle of condensation of factual material, unique in its range and close relation to terms of reference among medieval records. It gave an authoritative account of the land-holding position in 1086. In the twelfth century it became known as Domesday Book, because, just as at the Day of Judgement itself, no appeal was possible against its record. It was in a sense a feudal book, but its part in the creation of a national sentiment was also great, as the Norman settlement proved enduring. The description of the country was arranged shire by shire, but within each shire according to the holdings of the king and his tenants-in-chief, normally the ecclesiastical tenants first, followed by the lay tenants, from great Norman lords down to the few survivors in that rank of society from the Anglo-Saxon past. It has been estimated that only some four per cent of the landed wealth of England remained in Anglo-Saxon hands at tenant-in-chief level, though a significant number of Anglo-Saxon landlords survived as sub-tenants or lower down in the social scale. The new Norman or French-speaking lords became wealthy, some of tycoon status, as a result of their successful venture, and Domesday Book bears testimony to, and gives legal standing to their new wealth and tenures.

Though a feudal record, Domesday Book was created by processes deeply rooted in the English past: the authority of the shire court and the sheriff, the ability to take evidence on oath from the territorial units of hundred and vill. Domesday Book is a tribute to Norman energy and to Anglo-Saxon precedent, both feudal and territorial, and it is also proof of the nature of the great council as a body capable of initiating large-scale projects and carrying them through efficiently. Everyday business could not wait upon the summons and assembly of the great council, and for these executive and administrative aspects the Norman kings had to rely, like the Anglo-Saxons before them, on their household and a few close and trusted magnates, who would meet regularly around the court, the *curia regis*, as it was known. Final responsibility rested, as always, with the king. The court was peripatetic; men who sought judgments or administrative help had to seek the king and his court, whether it was in Normandy or in England. This peripatetic nature of the *curia* had one great effect on English institutional life. It became customary to select great officers of the king to act in the royal name in routine matters during the king's absence. Under William I the king's half-brother Odo of Bayeux (until his disgrace in 1082), Archbishop Lanfranc and Geoffrey, bishop of Coutances, from time to time exercised such special powers. Ranulf Flambard, later bishop of Durham, occupied a similar role in the reign of William II. It was in Henry I's time that this development reached its peak, and his principal ministerial bishop, Roger of Salisbury, became known as a capital justiciar, second only to the king. The office of justiciar as virtual head of the administration did not in fact develop in England, but the possibility of such development was plainly to be seen during these Norman generations.

Executive government developed along different and diffused lines. The royal court, the *curia regis*, proved fertile in experiment. Gradually, fixed offices and institutions grew up to cope with the three principal facets of government – the secretarial, the financial and the legal – but subject always to the overriding and undifferentiated power of the court. Secretarial developments were dominated by the emergence of the office of chancellor; the history of the office in England is continuous from the early days of William I. In the course of the later eleventh century a change in status came about. William's chancellors, in direct succession from the chief clerks of Edward the Confessor's writing office, were ministerial, of comparatively humble condition, anxious and pleased to receive high ecclesiastical office as their ultimate preferment away from the secretarial duties of the court. As business increased and as the influence of the office developed, there is a positive change, and bishops themselves became willing to receive promotion to the office of chancellor. Roger of Salisbury in the first part of the twelfth century consolidated the position. The chancellor became practical head of the active administration. The heart of his office rested in the custodianship of a royal seal with which royal acts would be authenticated and given the royal sanction. Roger also developed further rights and duties, and his presence in the royal council came to be taken for granted in the reign of Henry I. The chancellor was clearly regarded as of magnate status. Below him were a group, not numerous but very influential, of clerks in permanent government service. More or less permanent writing offices were established at great royal castles and palaces, notably at Winchester and at Westminster. By the end of the Norman period there was the nucleus of a permanent chancellor's department. The secretariat was well ordered.

More obvious and effective even than the secretarial developments were the developments on the financial side of government. The Normans inherited an efficient treasury for the collection and storing of money, and an efficient currency. They rapidly proved themselves very able indeed at the actual techniques of tax-collecting; the sources abound with comment on the severity of the gelds laid on the country. Norman activity involved experience and expertise on all sides. In the last decade of the eleventh century William Rufus relied heavily on Ranulf Flambard, the chief executor of the king's will, as he was termed. Roger of Salisbury performed even more onerous secretarial and financial duties for Henry I. The royal court remained an important financial centre, but more and more routine business was taken over by a specialized group of royal advisers, who in time came to be known as the barons of the Exchequer.

The Exchequer itself was a Norman innovation, first referred to in connection with the aid levied for the marriage of the king's daughter in 1110. Its principal functions were to act as an effective means of auditing accounts and to preserve records. The first roll of the Exchequer to survive comes from 1130, and the series is continuous from 1155 to the nineteenth century. The name 'exchequer' comes from the chessboard (*scaccarium*) arrangement into which the cloths used for checking and auditing accounts were divided. A full account of the workings of the Exchequer has been preserved from about 1170, and it is clear that the whole system of the Upper Exchequer and Lower Exchequer had by this date already taken on independent institutional life of its own. As an important step forward in the creation of permanent institutions of government, the Exchequer demands special emphasis. Efficient and permanent institutional life on the financial side contributed much to the making of England.

The Norman contribution to the creation of permanent judicial institutions was not quite so dramatic. Nevertheless, great advances were made in this field also. The royal court remained the undifferentiated source of judicial authority, but energetic reform, notably during the first decades of Henry I's reign, ensured the continuity in full vigour of the local courts of shire, hundred and *wapentake*. Not for nothing was Henry I known as the Lion of Justice. Norman kings employed freely the device of afforcing such local courts with the presence of close and trusted royal councillors to hear specific matters. Under the Conqueror both Odo of Bayeux and especially Geoffrey of Coutances often fulfilled this role, presiding over great pleas in the localities. The commissioners sent out to conduct the massive survey that resulted in Domesday Book possessed judicial powers that they used in some shires with full freedom. By the end of the eleventh century it was commonplace for royal judges to be sent to specific regions to hear pleas of special interest and importance to the king. In many shires a resident magnate took on the office of king's overseer of justice. Apart from judicial innovations in relation to finance and the court of the Exchequer, however, there was little trace of separate central differentiation of legal courts. The royal court remained the full royal court in the judicial sense. Special royal central judicial courts at fixed spots, and regular itinerant justices were an Angevin not a Norman achievement. The legal life of the community was carried on substantially through the old folk courts.

In these three fields of secretarial practice, finance and the administration of justice, great strides were nevertheless made during the Norman period. The full measure of Norman executive strength cannot be appreciated unless one outstanding achievement is brought into the balance. A true test of Norman success consists in the way they succeeded in articulating government, that is to say, in bringing the king's will into formidable touch with all the localities. The kingpin in Norman efforts in this direction was the officer known as the sheriff. The name of the sheriff was Saxon, shire reeve, and we have already seen how, because of developments in the late

Anglo-Saxon period, one of the shire reeves took on increasing responsibility for the government of the shire. The Normans treated the sheriff's office as the principal means by which they could govern. Initially, some of the most powerful men in the realm took on the role of sheriff; sometimes their authority extended over several shires. Much of Henry I's success came from his careful elevation of new men to the office of sheriff, and the sheriff became the principal royal representative in financial and judicial matters within the shire. Complaints concerning abuse of the office became increasingly vigorous and colourful. If a sheriff was also custodian of a royal castle, his control of a locality could be almost absolute. We praise the Normans for their administrative and governmental skill; without the energetic and powerful work of the sheriffs, the apparatus of Norman government would have been useless.

Executive government represents a major field in which the Normans contributed to the making of England. The giving to England of what was virtually a new aristocracy was an even deeper and more dramatic contribution. It was once common to describe the Norman Conquest and the subsequent settlement as one of the most successful takeover bids in Western European history; and there was much truth in the view. There was also, as some of our shrewdest observers have reminded us, an element of colonization in the process, though the limitations, too, of the colonizing enterprise have to be recognized. The Normans were for the most part rulers and governors, and it is only in the urban field that we have evidence for a strong influx of lesser folk in considerable numbers. Norman nobles, high churchmen, merchants and even some artisans thrived, but not Norman peasants as such; the Normans did not get their hands dirty in England. The facts of the settlement speak for themselves. The Normans could boast that no Englishman lost his lands merely because he was an Englishman, and in a sense they were right.

Duke William emphasized consistently the legality of his royal position as the true legal heir to his kinsman Edward the Confessor; Harold was rejected as an oathbreaker and a usurper. William was, nevertheless, in his attitude to law, to principles of land-holding and to the relationship of lord to man, essentially Norman, essentially

French, essentially Continental. He had saved himself and built up a strong feudal duchy in the north of France by firm insistence on his rights as feudal overlord within the territory of Normandy. He applied the same principles to his settlement of England. Those who had fought against him at Hastings and elsewhere were treated as rebels, and their lands declared forfeit. All landowners, indeed, were forced, as the Anglo-Saxon Chronicler said, to 'buy back their land' in the first year after the Conquest. An Englishman, no matter how wealthy or exalted in rank, found himself increasingly unable to fit into the new feudal framework; and in consequence, Englishmen of account tended to rebel. Within ten years of the Conquest virtually all political figures of importance and prominent land-owners were Norman or newcomers. In the church William acted more slowly and circumspectly, but he used the right of appoint-ment to such effect that by the end of his reign there was only one English bishop (Wulfstan of Worcester) and no English abbot.

Domesday Book bears witness to a wholesale process of Normani-zation among the aristocracy and landowning classes. The landed wealth of England rested in the hands of a small group of powerful tenants-in-chief, predominantly Norman and closely bound by ties of blood and of friendship to the king himself. Rivalries and inevitable tensions existed within this group, but for the first generation at least, in the face of outside pressures, the group retained an impressive solidarity. Their feeling of identification one with another was strengthened by the sheer activity of these great Norman lords. They were builders in the secular and ecclesiastical fields, and their castles and cathedrals remain impressive tributes to their energy and skill. They were cavalrymen or leaders of cavalry-men in a subjected country that was not proficient in the art. They were set apart from their subject peoples by language, custom and awareness of service to one of the great military chieftains of the day. Some of this solidarity, which arose from function as well as from feelings of social identification, began to loosen as the second generation appeared. Rivalry among the Conqueror's sons brought elements of faction prominently into the ruling class. The question of the political future of Normandy itself bred dissension and uncertainty. But the integrity never completely disappeared. The

Mowbrays, FitzOsberns, Montgomerys, Clares, Grandmesnils, Beaumonts, Mandevilles and their successors constituted a permanent and powerful new aristocratic and feudal element in English medieval life.

The aristocratic principle continued to manifest itself as a dominant feature throughout the reigns of Henry I and Stephen. Henry I's skill in the art of patronage kept them loyal to the crown, whilst Stephen's inadequacy in this vital direction led to disruption and civil war. The church, too, was absorbed into the feudal framework. All great tenants-in-chief, ecclesiastical as well as secular, held their land conditionally upon the service of so many knights for the king's host at fixed times and for fixed periods. The kings could and did also draw heavily on English financial resources to provide themselves with mercenary service and with feudal service above the stated customary service due; but the basic principles of obedience and promise of service helped beyond measure to keep the Norman aristocracy together as a tight-knit governing class. The abbot of Tavistock held his land in return for the provision of fifteen armed cavalrymen, fully equipped with necessary supporting infrastructure; and we know that the abbot alienated some of his most prosperous manors in the course of the succeeding generation in order to pay for this heavy burden of service. A powerful tenant-in-chief would hold his lands in return for a satisfactory performance of perhaps forty or even sixty knights, laced also with a degree of castle guard and general non-military service. The governors, by function as well as by race, language and custom, were thus drawn further away socially from their English subjects.

The very terms and incidents of feudal service helped to keep the ruling group together. A relief, amounting often to one year's rent or its equivalent, had to be paid to the overlord by a feudal tenant entering into his inheritance. On the marriage of a lord's eldest daughter or the knighting of his son, customary payment had to be made. These customs were already so important by the end of the eleventh century that they received a prominent position in the coronation charter of Henry I. Customs that applied to the king and his tenants-in-chief were also extended deeper and further down into the feudal hierarchy, so that the members of the whole ruling class, from king to tenant-in-chief to principal sub-tenants, consisting in time of what amounted to an honorial baronage, right down to the humble knight, felt themselves bound by a similarity of custom to match their military function. Only slowly and rarely did the English intrude into these top ranks of feudal society. The whole apparatus of government, and the rights and duties that went with it, remained solidly Norman and French during the greater part of the century after the Conquest. Only in the towns newly thriving under Norman discipline and peace did some Englishmen find and take their chance to prosper in this new energetic, bustling, class-ridden Norman world.

As we have already seen, the Norman period as a whole experienced three main persistent and interlocking political problems: the relationship with Normandy, the wider matters connected with other French possessions and the resultant ties with the Capetian king, and the question of succession. William I rejoiced in the new dignities and status that came to him as king of England, but his heart remained in Normandy, where he continued to spend much of his time and energy. He and his wife Matilda chose to be buried in the great churches that they had built at Caen. In the feudal world of the north of France he often appeared, notably when dissension broke out with his sons, little more than a powerful duke; the aura of majesty declined as he crossed the Channel. Within the wider French context, the incompetence and poor moral standing of King Philip I (1060–1106) undoubtedly helped him, but William had to fight hard to maintain his control of Brittany and Maine, and ultimately lost his life as a result of an injury suffered on campaign in the Vexin against his Capetian overlord. His horse stumbled, flinging him hard against the pommel of his saddle, and the resultant internal damage brought him to an agonizing death. He recognized that he had no hereditary right to England, but commended the kingdom to God with the stated wish that his son William might be chosen and that his reign be illustrious. Archbishop Lanfranc and a major part of the baronage saw that this wish was carried out. To his youngest son Henry William left 5000 pounds of money from the Treasury, and Henry lost no time in carefully weighing out the money and finding a safe place to deposit it. King William II spent much of his best energies re-establishing the practical unity of his father's dominions, taking full advantage of the chivalric Robert's crusading venture and using the superior financial resources of England to take the duchy into virtual pawn during Robert's absence in the Holy Land.

Another succession crisis occurred on the death of King William in the New Forest on 2 August 1100. The natural heir seemed to many the elder brother, Robert, now a crusading hero, but the younger brother Henry was on the spot, acted decisively, seized the Treasury, and was quickly crowned. His long reign of thirty-five years was divided politically into three phases. From 1100 to 1106 he was concerned with holding Robert in check and then in establishing personal control over Normandy. To strengthen his hand he effected a temporary reconciliation with Archbishop Anselm (in exile after a bitter quarrel with William II), and issued a charter of liberties that was to have a great influence on the later constitutional history of England. He also married Edith (who changed her name to Matilda on marriage), the daughter of Margaret, Queen of Scotland, and descendant of the old ruling Saxon house. From 1106 to 1120 he was chiefly concerned with stabilizing his position in the north of France, but then suffered a savage personal and diplomatic blow when his only legitimate son, William, died in the wreck of the White Ship. Much of his best diplomatic efforts in the last years of his reign, as we have seen, went to ensure the succession of his daughter Matilda, but in December 1135 Stephen of Blois, the king's nephew, for once acting with speed and decisiveness, succeeded to the Norman kingship.

Initially, Stephen's reign (1135–53) promised fair. He was supported by his brother, Henry of Blois, bishop of Winchester, issued a generous charter in favour of the church, and was well received by much of the baronage. Hasty action, the alienation of Normandy, and the unnecessary humiliation of Roger of Salisbury and the old guard, so to speak, of Henry I's administration quickly altered the scene. Matilda took her chance and, supported by her illegitimate half-brother Robert of Gloucester, set up a secure base in the West Country centred on Bristol – and so began a period of civil war. Politically, indeed, the reign of Stephen seemed by 1139 to be heading for disaster. In fact, general disaster was averted, though this is not to minimize the havoc caused by civil war and the disruption of the principles of authoritarian government set up by the early Norman rulers. In a great purple passage the Anglo-Saxon Chronicler, making his last composite entry in the Peterborough version of the Chronicle, gives a savagely gloomy view of the reign as a whole and also provides a glimpse of the deeper forces at work:

> When the traitors understood that he [King Stephen] was a mild man, and gentle and good, and did no justice, they perpetrated every enormity. They had done him homage, and sworn oaths, but they kept no pledge: all of them were perjured and their pledges nullified, for every powerful man built his castles and held them against him and they filled the country full of castles. When the castles were built they filled them with devils and wicked men.

There followed detailed horror stories of tortures inflicted on men and women to make them yield their wealth, of the exaction of 'protection money' on villages, of villages burnt, land untilled, starvation, emigration, complete disregard for ecclesiastical censure. The summing up is graphic:

> Whenever cultivation was done, the ground produced no corn because the land was all ruined by such doings, and they said openly that Christ and his saints were asleep. Such things, too much for us to describe, we suffered for nineteen years for our sins.

Modern historians have redressed some of the balance, pointing out that the anarchic conditions so described were confined in time and space. There were bad patches during the four years 1139–43 when the civil war was at its height and the forces evenly balanced. Most areas suffered from occasional violence, but truly atrocious anarchic conditions of the type described by the Chronicler were suffered principally in the eastern counties, where Geoffrey of Mandeville and his bullyboys held effective sway. Even so, the reign of Stephen was troubled and unhappy. Weak royal government had led to the growth of odious local tyranny. The Chronicler was right to emphasize in his account the lack of faith and the building of castles. Feudal order depended upon acceptance of the binding quality of oaths of fealty and the reciprocal rights and duties involved in the tie of homage. Respect for the church, the conscience of feudal society, was also a vital constituent in the creation of a rational order. Castles, without the restraining hand of royal authority with its inbuilt interest in law, quickly degenerated into instruments of tyranny.

England was ready and anxious to accept the strong rule of the Angevin Henry II after the discontents, uncertainties and occasional horrors of Stephen's reign. Another perceptive historian, Henry of Huntingdon, rejoiced in the accord made between Stephen and Henry in 1153, but reported accurately that the one serious moment of displeasure between them came when Duke Henry (as he was then) heard that the castles that had been constructed everywhere and put to evil uses had not been demolished in accordance with the treaty they had solemnly ratified. Many indeed had gone, but others, held by King Stephen's own followers, had been spared by the indulgence or duplicity of the king. One of Henry's first acts after his accession was to make sure that the so-called adulterine castles were demolished. Strong royal government demanded full control of castles, a vital element in the feudal order.

CHAPTER 6

The Angevin leap forward:
Henry II to Magna Carta

Although Stephen was the apparent victor of the civil war, it became obvious in the later years of his reign that his sons stood little chance of succeeding their father. The loss of Normandy to the Angevins proved decisive, and, as the young prince Henry grew and flourished in the Plantagenet Continental domains, more and more people in England looked hopefully to him for the future. A compromise was reached in 1153 after the death of Stephen's elder son. Henry was recognized as heir and, in 1154, he succeeded to the kingdom. He was already duke of Normandy (1150), count of Anjou (1151) and, as a result of his marriage to the formidable Eleanor (1152), duke of Aquitaine. The marriage took place on 18 May 1152, less than two months after the annulment of her previous marriage to the Capetian king Louis VII, 'more monk than king', as she is reputed to have complained. England was confirmed as an integral part of a great French-speaking complex of territories sometimes known as the Angevin or Norman empire.

The succeeding sixty-two years, 1154–1216, have a rich unity of their own, impressed by the powerful personalities of the Angevin rulers Henry II (1154–89) and his sons Richard I, the Lionheart (1189–99), and then John (1199–1216). They were a turbulent lot, energetic and given to outbursts of violence. Walter Map praised Henry II for his affable, friendly qualities but had to confess that 'impatient of repose, he did not scruple to disturb half Christendom'. Richard I's soldierly qualities were never in doubt, but contemporaries varied in their estimates of his character, though agreeing substantially on his hot temper, his generosity and his love of music. More attention has been paid by historians, contemporary and later, to John's character than perhaps to that of any other medieval monarch. Excavation of his tomb in Worcester cathedral in 1797 has even given us an accurate physical description of the man, five foot and five inches in height and rather stout. Ceaseless energy, restless movement, impulsive reactions appear to have been dominant elements in his make-up. He could be cruel and yet also compassionate, deeply vain and self-interested, and yet able to strive after efficiency in government and a sense of justice in legal matters. The royal mother, Eleanor of Aquitaine, lived on into her seventies into the reign of John and was a considerable influence on both her sons. It was Richard who was said to have declared that 'from the devil we came and to the devil we shall return'. Harsh, glittering, impulsive and fast-moving men they undoubtedly were; the sin of *accidie*, laziness, could never be laid at their doorstep.

The men matched the times. The main political events stand out with sharp clarity. A savage crisis in the relationship between church and state erupted in the 1160s, which resulted in the exile of Archbishop Thomas Becket and his subsequent murder in his own cathedral of Canterbury on 29 December 1170. The conflict came about on general issues, the attempt to frame the customs of the English church in writing by the Constitutions of Clarendon (1164), and the specific matter of the criminous clerks: should a man be tried twice for the same offence? To the European world, and especially to the papacy, it must all have appeared somewhat old-fashioned. General issues were in fact overshadowed by the bitter hostility between two powerful men, Henry II and Thomas Becket, who had been his friend, companion and chancellor. Even if the exact words enshrined in popular myth and attributed to Henry II were never spoken – 'Who will rid me of this turbulent priest?' – the sentiments were certainly such; and the four knights who crossed the Channel to kill the archbishop, Reginald FitzUrse, William de Tracy, Hugh de Morville and Richard le Bret, acted as if on their royal master's business. The horror of the murder and the bravery of the archbishop were universally recognized. Becket was quickly sanctified; Henry II performed public penance. Legends spread concerning the murderers as well as the saint, and pilgrimages to the shrine at Canterbury multiplied as the cathedral itself was rebuilt in the new Gothic style. The creation of a national saint did much to bind the community of England at its grass roots. Becket was remembered as a native Londoner as well as a great churchman.

Family quarrels disturbed the otherwise aggressive Angevin political success of the 1170s and 1180s. In 1173 a revolt led by Eleanor and her sons involved virtually all the rivals of Henry II in the Anglo-French world, including the French and Scottish kings. Henry's wealth, recruitment of mercenaries, and sheer luck preserved his control. Ten years later an almost equally severe family quarrel nearly led to a similar situation, averted in fact by the sudden death in June 1183 of the young king Henry, who had led the revolt against his father in company with his brother Geoffrey of Brittany, the Capetian king Philip II, Raymond of Toulouse and Hugh of Burgundy. Henry II lamented bitterly the treachery of his sons. Richard turned against him at the end, but even so, in July 1189 the Angevin inheritance was transmitted intact to Richard as the eldest surviving son.

The Third Crusade dominated the early years of Richard's reign. His reputation as a crusader was well deserved even though he did not succeed in regaining Jerusalem, and his capture on his way home by Duke Leopold of Austria and subsequent ransom entered firmly into the national myth. In exaggerated form, his reign reveals the intensity of the growth of English government even in the king's absence. As for King John (1199–1216), lacking his father's skill and his brother's military valour and reputation, he suffered early political defeat at the hands of the Capetian king Philip II (Augustus) and by 1204 was thrown back substantially on his English lands. Attempts to regain his French patrimony ended in failure, consummated by the defeat of his ally Otto IV, the German emperor, at Bouvines in July 1214. Relationships with the church grew tempestuous after John's failure to impose John de Gray, bishop of Norwich, on the archiepiscopal throne at Canterbury. Pope Innocent III proceeded to consecrate Stephen Langton at Viterbo on 17 July 1207, and England was placed under an interdict from 1208 to 1212. King John himself was excommunicated and eventually was forced, under threat of invasion and rebellion, to submit. In May 1213 John resigned his kingdoms of England and Ireland to Innocent III, paid homage and swore fealty to the pope, and further promised a tribute of 1000 marks a year, 700 for England and 300 for Ireland. Later critics railed at John for these actions, but the immediate consequences were advantageous to him. Bitter hostility had developed in England, partly because of John's oppressive government, partly through his lack of political success in France. In the struggles of his last years, which resulted in the emergence of two great political figures, William Marshall and Archbishop Stephen Langton, and the issue of Magna Carta in June 1215, John could rely on the consistent support of the powerful pope.

All these political dramas – the murder of Becket, the Third Crusade, the loss of Normandy, Magna Carta – highlight the significance of the late twelfth and early thirteenth centuries in the making of England. Yet the true elements that were beginning to shape a coherent community were to be found at a lower level of society, in the manors, hundreds, shires and townships – there the wealth was generated that made successful government possible – and in the new universities of Oxford and Cambridge.

The Angevin period, as it is sometimes called, was indeed a time of economic expansion in country and in town. The Norman peace had had a steadying effect on economic life; with the Angevins the process went further. Slavery, already out of tune with advanced legal thought, gradually diminished, though the peasantry found itself subject to the imposition of increasingly heavy labour service. High inflation between 1180 and 1220 brought substantial changes to the countryside. The high farming of the Middle Ages, where more and more tenants-in-chief and sub-tenants exploited the demesne to their own advantage, intensified. Labour service and feudal dues grew more burdensome, and life became harder for whole sections of the population. The forest laws came to be regarded as a symptom of royal high-handedness; it is no accident that many legendary stories concerning Robin Hood tend to be concentrated on the reign of King John towards the height of the inflationary pressure.

In the town as in the country there is evidence for an increase in population and prosperity. London grew so that its population reached at least 20,000 by the end of the twelfth century, and some good critics think the figure may have been substantially higher. A lively description of the city, written 1170–83 as a preface to his life of Thomas Becket, was given by William FitzStephen. He painted an idyllic picture of the city, 'happy in the healthiness of its air, its observance of Christian practice, the strength of its fortifications, its natural situation, the honour of its citizens, and the modesty of its matrons'. There were 3 great churches (St Paul's, St Martin's and Holy Trinity), 13 conventual churches, and 126 lesser parish churches. The suburbs were pleasant, the schools notable and the food excellent. A full account was given of the sports of London, including a primitive sort of skiing when the great marsh 'that washes the north wall of the city is frozen over'. The only plagues of London were said to be the immoderate drinking of fools and the frequency of fires. A contrary view was given in a passage in the chronicle of Richard of Devizes, monk of Winchester, where a French Jew gives advice during the reign of Richard I of which towns to visit and which not. London is at the top of the list of dangerous places, and he sums it all up by saying 'therefore if you do not wish to live with evil-doers [cum turpibus] do not live in London'! Not surprisingly, Winchester appears at the other end of the scale. Other towns mentioned, mostly with unflattering asides, are Canterbury, Rochester, Chichester, Oxford, Exeter, Bath, Worcester, Hereford, Ely, Durham, Norwich, Lincoln and Bristol.

For the most part, the king and the lords of the boroughs retained the control they needed to ensure that they took their full share of the wealth of the urban communities, but the general move was towards an elaboration of the conception of a free borough and towards a degree of self-government in the towns. A decisive period of change came in the last decade of the twelfth century and the reign of John, triggered and accelerated by inflationary pressures. London, as always, was ahead of other towns and achieved in 1191 the status of a commune. The office of mayor evolved about this time, and for a period of some twenty years a remarkable man, Henry FitzAilwin, guided the affairs of the city, winning concessions that permitted Londoners the key right to appoint their own sheriffs. A series of royal charters from John further strengthened their position. King John attempted to play on internal tensions within the city, but an oligarchy of rich patrician families remained effectively in control, winning for themselves a special position both in the preparatory stages of the conflict between John and his barons and in Magna Carta itself. Permission to elect a mayor annually in place of tenure for life was granted to London in 1215. At the very time when Hubert Walter and his successors were building up Westminster as a permanent seat for the government of England, London was putting its own house in order and laying the foundations for the growth of its permanent institutions: the mayoralty, the shrievalty and the court of aldermen.

Elsewhere, the same process of clarification can be discerned as the proliferation of charters intensifies, notably during the reign of John. The royal hand remained firm, and charters could be withdrawn as regularly as they could be granted, but the trend was towards recognition of a degree of self-government, permission to elect a mayor or a council of the more discreet and responsible men, to elect coroners who would keep the pleas of the crown, and a town council. Towns, even the greatest, were still within the basic administrative structures of the realm, generally subordinate to the shire, but if they farmed their own taxes, enjoyed the privileges of guild merchants, elected aldermen and appointed leading citizens to help the bailiffs collect tax, they were well on the way to achieving corporate status and dignity, which could not be ignored if royal government were to be efficient. Revealing and variable detail may be found in charters for boroughs such as Hereford, Gloucester, Shrewsbury, Ipswich, Northampton and Lincoln, as well as in many lesser urban centres.

It is important to recognize that borough privileges, rights and duties were becoming accepted as such a standard feature of material life that grants could be made in perpetuity (certainly after 1199) of the rights of a 'free borough', or 'with all liberties and free customs which our free boroughs have in all things well and in peace', or 'with all liberties and customs pertaining to a free borough and to a market or fair'. Sometimes a particular borough, new or old, was to enjoy the liberties of another borough, which they themselves could chose: so King's Lynn chose Oxford (which in turn enjoyed many of the liberties of London), and Burton-on-Trent was left free to choose those of any neighbouring borough. Such growth of a widespread awareness of how towns should be governed, and of how taxation should be collected from them, did much to consolidate feelings of social unity within the English community.

Town government is one thing, urban prosperity quite another. A possible index to the question of prosperity comes in the fortunes of the Jewish community in England. Introduced at the time of the Norman Conquest from a Rouen base as an offshoot of French Jewry, they flourished in their own quarters very much under royal protection, and exercised an essential function in a developing community – the handling of finance that involved inter-community transactions, rejected by the Christians as usurious. Hatred was stirred up against them from time to time, the most notorious incidents associated with accusation of ritual murder and defiling the sacraments. The story of the martyrdom of the little boy William, St William of Norwich, in 1144 was the most notorious of these incidents. The coronation of Richard I, together with the fervour, not to say fanaticism, of the Third Crusade, prompted the worst outbreak of pogroms known in the country in London, Lynn, Norwich, Lincoln, Stamford, and above all York, where some 150 Jewish men, women and children perished, reputedly by self-immolation, rather than submit to the mercies of the mob. Other towns, such as Hereford, also possessed a substantial Jewish population. They were taxed by the king more or less at will, and King John in particular exacted huge sums from them in fines and tallages. A special Exchequer of the Jews was set up at Westminster to deal with Jewish affairs. Their part in financing large-scale enterprises, the building of great cathedrals and abbeys, the equipment of armed forces and arrangements for continued finances overseas, can scarcely be exaggerated. As the chief financial experts, they give proof of a degree of urban maturity, of cosmopolitan activity, and also of concentration of Angevin political effort in England.

The Angevin period was a critical period also in the political development of the English nation. Under Henry II and Richard I links with the Continent were at their strongest. We think rightly of Henry II as one of the most powerful English kings, but more than half his time was spent in France. Richard was in England for a few months for his coronation in 1189 and again in 1194, but that was all.

119

French was the language of the court and of the aristocracy; French cultural life flourished, while English as a literary language sank further into the background. The Peterborough Chronicle had its last entry in 1155. The copying of Anglo-Saxon manuscripts, still a substantial activity in many monasteries up to about 1150, declined in quality and quantity. Only in the West Midlands is there clear evidence of important creative work in English with Layamon's *Brut* (*c*.1200) and the devotional literature *Ancrene Wisse* and *Ancrene Riwle*. French *chansons de geste* and then *romans d'aventur* were the reading matter of the sophisticated groups in courts and towns. Stories of Arthur, his knights and the Round Table outrivalled the stories of Charlemagne and his paladins on both sides of the Channel, and became central to the imagination and increasingly chivalric sentiments of the age. The 'matter of Britain' in the wider sense represented the creation of an acceptable pre-history of Britain: Brutus and Trojan antecedents, King Lear, Gorboduc, Julius Caesar, Cymbeline, Constantine and Maximianus, as well as Arthur. The discovery of the tombs of Arthur and Guinevere at Glastonbury in 1191 was as illuminating in its way as the murder of Becket in 1170. At first sight the notion of Englishness seemed very much to be thrust into the background, but this impression is deceptive. The British ideal served the needs and ambitions of the English monarchy. The same may be said of the involvement with France. Henry II spent much of his political energy there, governing more of historic France directly than the Capetian king himself, arranging for his sons to succeed to lucrative fiefs (Richard to Aquitaine, Geoffrey to Brittany), curbing or failing to curb their ambition and their violence. But the heart of his government and his finances lay in prosperous England.

At the same time, interest in St Denis and the oriflamme, the legends of Charlemagne, Roland and Oliver fastened the sentiment of Frenchness on the Continent. Philip Augustus succeeded in 1180 and took advantage first of Angevin squabbles and then of Richard Lionheart's absence on crusade to build up Paris as the natural fulcrum of the northern intellectual world. After Richard's death and John's succession, the way was clear for a dramatic show of political strength on the part of the French king. Philip Augustus asserted his feudal rights, summoned King John to answer for feudal misdeeds and, on his failure to appear before a French court, was able to treat him as a contumacious vassal. In 1204 John was driven from the bulk of his Continental possessions by force. The loss of Normandy – for that was felt by most to be the precious unit – led to a simplification of loyalties among the landholders. John's subsequent failure to reclaim his lands contributed to massive unrest and to the forced issue of Magna Carta. From the English point of view the resolution of the tangled Continental situation proved a positive advantage. The upper classes remained French in language, culture and sympathies, but their wealth, their landed authority, their political strength, came to rest on their English lands and rights.

The same Angevin period experienced important formative developments within the British context. In Scotland, the main concern of the kings of England was to insist, whenever conditions were favourable, on a degree of subordination from the Scottish crown. The chief political objective was to establish a peaceful and stable border. In July 1157 King Malcolm IV met Henry II, did homage to him and in return received the earldom of Huntingdon. Malcolm's brother and successor William the Lion (1165–1214) rashly joined the great rebellion of 1173–4 against Henry, was defeated, captured and forced to agree to terms that involved him in doing homage for Scotland and all his other lands, swearing fealty, and yielding stated castles and hostages.

Even at this, one of the lowest points in Scottish royal history, there was no attempt to depose him or to dispossess him of castles north of the Forth. Henry, indeed, adopted a friendly attitude towards Scotland, and Richard on his accession was more anxious to exact money from the Scottish king than to prosecute any theatrical claim to overlordship. Roger Howden, a good historian with direct access to important events, reported that the king of the Scots (i.e. William) performed homage to King Richard for the holding of his dignities in England, as the kings of Scots, his predecessors, were accustomed to hold them, and that Richard quitclaimed him and all his heirs for ever from all allegiance and subjection for the kingdom of Scotland. Richard's concern was to collect as much money as possible for his crusade. King William paid him ten thousand good

Scottish marks, and in return the English king was pleased to slacken the ties of lordship and, indeed, to leave the way open for a reassertion of a Scottish claim to an earldom of Northumbria. John was more severe in his dealings with Scotland and in 1209 forced an agreement on the now aged King William, which exacted hostages and a large cash payment, imposed marriage settlements and involved a weakening of the Scottish claim to the northern earldom. Record of the marriage settlements is as elusive as the settlements themselves. It is likely that John had intentions to arrange a marriage for his infant son Henry when he came of age, but in the event the three daughters of King William married great English magnates: Hubert de Burgh, earl of Kent, Roger Bigod, earl of Norfolk, and Gilbert Marshall, earl of Pembroke.

The play and counterplay of English and Scottish interests during this period was considerable. When England was in the ascendant, claims were made for homage that would place the northern kingdom in feudal subjection to the English crown. When English interest diminished or preoccupation became too great elsewhere, Scottish independence was stressed, accompanied by claims to a northern earldom (possibly for the heir to the Scottish throne), to the earldom of Huntingdon and to rights of hospitality within England. There was no attempt whatsoever on the part of the Angevins to deny the internal integrity of the Scottish crown. Scotland was a kingdom in a degree of subordination to England, according to political circumstance. From the pure Scottish point of view, the native Scottish, the threats came not from direct English aggression but in much more subtle fashion from internal pressures within the kingdom. The king and much of the aristocracy aimed at a twelfth-century cosmopolitanism that put them more at home with the Anglo-Norman establishment within England than with their own folk. Military feudalism became significant in Scotland during the reign of David I (1124–53), but it was precisely during the Angevin period and especially under William the Lion (1165–1214) that it intensified and became the normal relationship by which the greater lay tenants held their land. William's mother was Ada de Warenne, of the great Anglo-Norman feudal family; and some of the Warenne vassals, the Giffards, the St Martins, the Norman

Balliols, settled in the northern kingdom. The Bruces, the Stewarts and the Morvilles were already there. By the end of the century the military aristocracy was hard to distinguish from their cousins further south, bound by ties of blood, marriage and *mores* to the ruling groups in the wider Angevin world.

The Welsh situation was different. As a result of the reign of Stephen, the native Welsh princes found themselves in a stronger political position than at any time since the Norman Conquest of England. They were too near home for full independence to be tolerated, and their leadership was of a different nature from the Scottish, with its long-established traditions of unitary kingship. The Welsh naturally wished to retain their own social structures, laws and language, but sheer military force meant that their realistic hopes were bound sooner or later to involve recognition of a degree of feudal dependence and client status to the English king. The great Marcher lords formed a further vital element in the political equation, and they and their kinsfolk were too intimately woven into the ruling inner circles of English political life for there to be much effective hope of widespread and permanent native Welsh independent rule.

Henry II recognized the problem early in his reign, and in 1157–8 launched an expedition which John of Salisbury described as 'an attempt to conquer the Welsh amidst their Alps and sub-Alps'. The most powerful Welsh prince, Owain Gwynedd (1137–70), performed homage and was forced to yield hostages and territory in the north-east of Wales. Henry continued to play on the theme of feudal overlordship. Another strong prince emerged in the south in the person of Rhys ap Gruffudd (1158–97), the Lord Rhys, as he came to be known. At Woodstock in July 1163 Owain Gwynedd, Rhys and five of the greater men from Wales performed homage not only to Henry II, but also to his son and, at that stage, potential successor, Prince Henry. There was, however, no resulting immediate peace, and the late 1160s were turbulent. The death of Owain Gwynedd, the acute embarrassment caused by the murder of Thomas Becket at Canterbury in December 1170 and, most important of all in this respect, the hiving off of much of the energy of the Anglo-Normans and Flemings from Pembrokeshire into their Irish ventures, brought

123

about a radical change in affairs. In his recent authoritative analysis
Professor Rees Davies describes the whole period 1172–1277 as an
age of consolidation and definition. A broad equilibrium of power
had been achieved and was substantially to persist, certainly until
well into the reign of King John. The key figure was the Lord Rhys,
who became the firm ally of King Henry and was appointed justiciar
of South Wales. Most of the lordships recovered by Welsh princes
after 1135 (the notable exceptions were Carmarthen and Oswestry)
remained under Welsh control. Much of the lowland area of South
Wales was finally under Anglo-Norman rule. Royal Angevin policy
was not to conquer but to insist on the reality of feudal dependence,
with its resulting obligations in men, money and provender.

After 1169–70 attitudes towards Wales were very much con-
ditioned by the need to retain firm and permanent control of the sea
routes to Ireland. In Welsh terms this meant strong physical
presence in the ports of Cardiff, Swansea and Milford Haven, with
formidable back-up in the lordships of Glamorgan, Gower, and
above all Pembroke, where the Marshall family came to dominate.
William Marshall himself became earl of Pembroke in 1189 on his
marriage to Isabella, heiress of Richard Strongbow, conqueror of
Leinster (d. 1176), and assumed responsibility for the massive
refortification of Pembroke castle. Henry II, at first reluctant to be
involved directly in Ireland, quickly seized the chances offered by
Strongbow's success. By the end of his reign the Angevin hold was
sufficient for Ireland to be portioned to his youngest son, *dominus
Hiberniæ* – a title that continued to be used by succeeding generations of English kings to the time of Henry VIII, who assumed the
style king of Ireland in 1542.

The tensions and inconsistencies inherent in the Angevin situation become clear the more we ponder the relationship with Wales,
Scotland and Ireland. At no time did England seem more sub-
merged in an Anglo-French cosmopolitan European world, and yet
the shape of movement towards an English-dominated Britain is
also visible. The larger political scene can, however, mislead.
Angevin genius expressed itself most strongly in its detailed appli-
cation to the business of government and administration. The
Normans had provided the skeleton of settlement, colonization,

exploitation of landed wealth; the Angevins contributed the solid flesh of permanent institutional government. This was true in detail of all the territories they came to govern, not in any standardized pattern, but with variations dependent on regional experience. Nowhere was the ground more fertile and better prepared for the growth of efficient government than in England. Under Henry II and his sons England became something of a model feudal monarchy. Over-emphasis on royal authority led to baronial erup- tion and the formulation of ideas of the rule of law in Magna Carta, but the great charter itself was a royal charter and in no way rejected the basic principles of monarchy. Angevin achievements proved permanent and enduring in the fields of administration, record-keeping and, above all else, in law.

Angevin skill in administration has long been a commonplace. This is not to say that the twelfth-century kings were businessmen in any modern sense. Nothing could be further from the truth; they were soldiers, huntsmen, outdoor men whose success depended on straightforward powers of leadership in an aggressively male mili- tary world. Their reputations depended also, however, on their ability to appoint good subordinates, make good judgments, and take good counsel. Yet personal though their authority might be (they were truly kings), not even the energetic Henry II could cope personally with the flood of business that converged on the royal court. He had increasingly to rely on subordinates, ecclesiastical and secular, and on institutions growing up initially around the royal court but tending to take on independent lives of their own. This was especially true in the field of finance, the work of the secretariat, the judiciary and local government.

The upper court of the Exchequer provided the motor force behind financial organization in Angevin England. From 1160 to about 1180 an extraordinary man, prototype of the medieval King's Remembrancer and our later superior Treasury higher civil servants, Thomas Brown by name, dominated the court as direct representative of the king. With experience in Sicily behind him, he drew on knowledge of the most advanced accounting techniques known to twelfth-century Europe. Under his guidance the court came to meet at a fixed place, normally Westminster, at Easter and

Michaelmas. Its primary function was to authenticate the sheriffs' accounts as they delivered royal revenues, but there quickly developed elements of general business. In the king's absence, an important officer known as a justiciar presided. There was inevitably a degree of overlap with the king's household, his chamber and wardrobe. Because of the strong element of routine annual collection and accounting, the record-keeping element in the Exchequer quickly became important. From 1155 the series of Rolls of the Exchequer, recording the receipt of moneys from the sheriffs, is continuous. The main Treasury, initially at Westminster, operated as the dispensing agent of the king and royal government. Regular audit and record-keeping enabled the inner councillors of the king to keep a firm check on royal finance and also, sometimes directly sometimes indirectly, on the general business of the realm. Even in the inflationary circumstances of the early thirteenth century, the officers of the king tried to maintain accurate and helpful records.

The secretarial side of the government was closely bound up with the administration of finance and law. The king's frequent absences from England left much authority in the hands of great officers of the crown, commonly called justiciars. They exercised their delegated authority through the administrative machinery of the Exchequer, sometimes in harmony with, and sometimes in rivalry with other great officers, notably the chancellors. At this stage of development there was always the possibility that decisions could be overthrown at a word direct from the king, even if the king himself were miles away across the Channel. Great offices held by powerful officers helped to cement the sentiment of England as a unitary kingdom. But they provided no check on monarchy; the officers were royal servants. They were nevertheless very powerful men and very able men, who built up a formidable administrative tradition in the second half of the twelfth century. Thomas Becket himself was chancellor (1155–62) before he became archbishop of Canterbury; Robert de Beaumont and Richard de Lucy brought prestige and authority to the office of justiciar in the 1160s and 1170s, but it was in the last decades of the century that the administrative satraps reached new heights. Ranulf Glanville may or may not have written the great treatise on the laws and customs of England attributed to him, but he certainly dominated the stable English administrative structures during his term as sole justiciar, 1180–9. His career reminds us of the type of man we are dealing with, capable of playing a full part in the life of the court and military establishment, as well as the legal and administrative offices. Sheriff of York in 1163, he was removed from office as a result of the great Inquest of Sheriffs in 1170 but quickly recouped his fortunes. In 1174 he captured the Scottish king in battle, and promotion followed to the status of royal judge and then justiciar. He died in Acre in 1191 on campaign with Richard Lionheart.

The greatest of all these Angevin administrators, Hubert Walter, received much of his training in Glanville's household (and indeed some scholars think that he may have been chiefly responsible for Glanville's *Tractatus*). Walter came to dominate English administration at a peculiarly delicate time, with an absentee king, Richard I, first on crusade and then in an Austrian prison. Faced with the challenge of raising the king's ransom, he achieved that formidable task, tightening the financial machinery and innovating in the process. He was a cleric: bishop of Salisbury (1189–93) and archbishop of Canterbury (1193–1205); he held both the great offices of state: justiciar under Richard (1193–8), chancellor under John (1199–1205). And he did not stand alone; William Longchamp, bishop of Ely (1189–97), though deprived of much of his authority in 1191, remained chancellor and was no mere cipher; Geoffrey FitzPeter succeeded Hubert Walter as justiciar in July 1198, and remained in office until his death in 1213. Between them, though with Hubert Walter as the principal creative mind behind it all, these men and their clerks and followers established an enduring routine secretarial practice that did much to bind the community together. Regular records were kept at Chancery in the form of continuous enrolments. Administrative precedents were laid down that were to bear fruit in the creation of permanent institutions. A small seal for use in administration was a product of the ingenuity of Henry II's advisers, but received full recognition as an instrument of regular royal government – a private seal, or privy seal – in the early years of the reign of King John.

By the very nature of the business transacted, separate institutional life was not as much in evidence on the secretarial side of government as on the financial. The royal court and royal household remained the principal generating agencies, and from the reign of Henry II men trained in the royal chamber became the backbone of the administration, with a regular criss-cross of membership and activity between household, chancery, chamber and wardrobe in secretarial matters. Clerical skills were high, and clerical rewards (in the full ambiguity of English usage of the term 'clerical') were also considerable. The first episcopal appointments of Richard I's reign, made at Pipewell in September 1198, were all four of them drawn from the *curia*: Godfrey de Lucy to Winchester, Richard FitzNeal, the treasurer, to London, William Longchamp, the chancellor, to Ely, and Hubert Walter to Salisbury. High standards were imposed on penmanship and drafting to royal records, and efficient chancery clerks employed. Charters, writs and royal letters were carefully written, and the distinction, so important for later government, was already made between letters patent (that is to say letters open for all to see) and letters close (which were addressed to individuals and issued carefully folded or rolled into a cylinder and sealed by the small seal). By 1201 letters patent were enrolled and eventually subdivided into specific areas or topics of long-standing concern: Norman, Gascon, Treaty Rolls and the like; Close Rolls were enrolled, certainly from 1204. The chancery also evolved methods of recording payments, final concords, and information relating to complicated financial transactions for future reference. Inefficiency, violence, arbitrary actions subsisted, but the official records of John's reign give full evidence of a degree of reality in the concept of the territorial kingdom of England.

There remains what in many respects constitutes the most impressive aspect of Angevin government: the question of law and the judiciary, and legal organization generally. Henry II is recognized as one of the great legal innovators in English history and has even been called the true founder of the Common Law, though the characteristics of the man that impressed contemporaries were sheer animal energy, will to govern, and hot temper. Responsibility for the death of his own archbishop, marital quarrels, bitter conflict with his sons sat uneasily with the solemnity of Common Law.

26 Chepstow castle: the lower courses represent part of FitzOsbern's work
(d. 1071) at the strategic crossing point where the Wye meets the Severn.

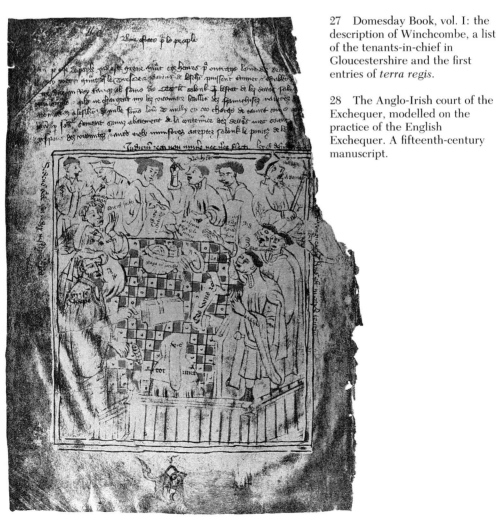

27   Domesday Book, vol. I: the description of Winchcombe, a list of the tenants-in-chief in Gloucestershire and the first entries of *terra regis*.

28   The Anglo-Irish court of the Exchequer, modelled on the practice of the English Exchequer. A fifteenth-century manuscript.

29 An eleventh-century illustration of punishment in prison and in the stocks.

30 An illustration of lawlessness from a thirteenth-century Life of Edward the Confessor.

31 Royal officers receiving taxation: from the Eadwine Psalter, a Canterbury manuscript at Trinity College, Cambridge.

32 The south porch of Kilpeck church, Herefordshire: mid-twelfth century, with elaborate stone carving reminiscent of Anglo-Scandinavian sculptural styles.

33 Twelfth-century wall-painting from Claverley in Shropshire.

34 St Mary's church, Iffley, Oxfordshire: a fine example of a twelfth-century Romanesque church.

35 Lanfranc, archbishop of Canterbury, 1070–89, from a twelfth-century manuscript of his tract *De corpore et sanguine domini*, directed against the teachings of Berengar of Tours.

36   The martyrdom of Becket: a wall-painting of *c*.1200, from Bramley church, Hampshire.

37   Canterbury cathedral, looking east to the unique circular corona, an outstanding achievement of later twelfth-century architecture by William of Sens and William the Englishman.

38, 39 The great seal of Henry II.

40 The tomb of Richard I at Fontevrault.

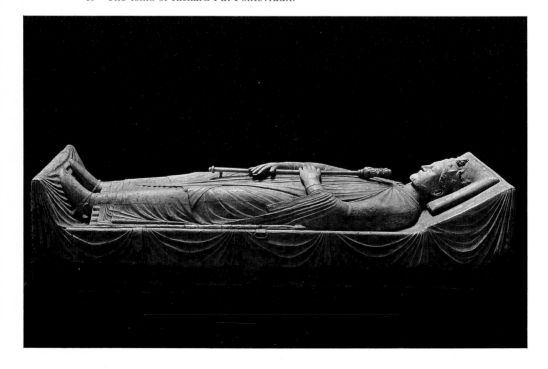

There are elements of incongruity in Henry's character and, certainly, as far as courts of law are concerned, we must be careful not to attribute too much in the way of institutional creation to him. Pressure of business and the help of some of the most learned men of the day enabled him to set up in about 1178 a permanent court, normally at Westminster, which was to hear pleas in the king's absence. But there was no clear line of demarcation between it and the *curia regis* in any of its attributes. The phrase 'king's court' could still be used loosely to describe the great council, the smaller council in the presence of the king, or the court of the Exchequer, which was by no means limited to financial affairs in its sessions. To seek justice at such a court was an expensive business and tended to remain a privilege of the landowning class. Other steps were needed to meet the flood of litigious activity so characteristic of the later twelfth century.

The Angevins aimed to meet this need by making royal justice more efficient and cheaper, and by fastening firmly a system of royal itinerant justices on to the structure of the old shire courts. Earlier in the century Henry I had employed such men with great effect on an *ad hoc* basis. His grandson Henry II now moved towards a more systematic organization of such judicial visitations in the form of regular circuits, or eyres. In 1176 eighteen justices were sent out to the shires on six separate circuits to ensure that some of the general enactments of the Assize of Northampton were carried out. Similar arrangements were made later in Henry's reign. Folk courts and royal justices were now firmly melded into one coherent institution. The jurisdiction exercised by the itinerant justices was more closely defined and therefore more circumscribed than the virtually limitless powers of the central courts, but it was still royal justice. As administrative officers as well as judicial, they did much to bring a sense of unity to England, supervising the sheriffs, investigating malpractices, fining shire courts for faulty judgments, enforcing fiscal claims, and freely articulating government by their direct transmission of royal orders to county and hundred courts.

Common Law under the Angevins became an instrument for the unification of England for two other principal reasons. Procedures already used by the Normans and rooted in Anglo-Saxon custom were sharpened, so that they became part and parcel of the routine legal custom of the land. The writ, as we have already seen, was a simple and effective means of making the royal will known. Henry II, intent on safeguarding the peace and anxious to provide remedies that would avoid turbulent squabbles over land, had his lawyers establish *pro forma* writs that could be sued out of the royal chancery. The writ *mort d'ancestor* permitted a claimant to summon an assize at which twelve lawful men would answer directly whether a claimant's ancestor had died seized of the land in question and whether the claimant was the next heir. It is likely that this writ originated in decisions taken at the Assize of Northampton in 1176. Ten years earlier at the Assize of Clarendon (1166) an even more famous writ may have originated, the writ of *novel disseisin*, though it is possible that as a regular process in civil law it postdated *mort d'ancestor*. A great future awaited *novel disseisin*. To all appearances the simplest of the possessory remedies, it enabled a man dispossessed of his free tenement unjustly and without judgment to have recourse to a royal writ. Decision would be reached on the question of whether the claimant had been newly 'disseised', or dispossessed, of his free tenement. Litigation about church property, specifically about the right of advowson, or presentation to a living, could also be dealt with through an action initiated in the royal court by a writ of *darrein presentement*, under the terms of which the question to be decided was who had presented to the benefice on the occasion of the last vacancy.

There is a vast literature on all these writs. The great legal historian F.W. Maitland stressed rightly that they were practical, that they were royal, convenient and rational. They provided reasonable alternatives to the more cumbersome procedures associated with the writ of right, grand assizes, and procedures that could lead to trial by battle. Modern scholars have tempered some of the enthusiasm for the so-called possessory assizes. It is possible that Maitland did not allow sufficiently for the law of courts other than the royal. Yet his main analysis remains firm, and, from the point of view of those struggling to see the emergence of a permanent identity in England, the analysis is vital. The possessory assizes might often, as modern views would stress, deal with disputes between lord and tenant, as much as between neighbour and neighbour. They show clearly, nevertheless, at grass-roots level how practical expression was given to the notion of the king as the source of redress of wrong in basic matters that concerned the legitimate possession of land. As they are safeguarded in Magna Carta, it is no accident that the writs and the assizes that derived from them, especially *novel disseisin*, increased in popularity in the thirteenth century as the feudal monarchy of England developed into a strong territorial kingdom.

If the writs, with all that they implied in the summons of assizes and increased convenience of royal justice, represented one element in Angevin law of permanent importance, even more significant was a second element consequent on – though not exclusively so – the possessory assizes: the increased use of juries. It is substantially true that the ordinances of Henry II introduced trial by jury as part of the normal machinery of civil justice. Older methods of proof were not abolished; indeed, proof by battle remained technically possible until 1819, and proof by oath-helpers, astonishingly, until 1833. But increasingly, suits were settled by twelve good men and true, acting not as witnesses but as judges on a precise point of fact. Parallel developments took place in criminal cases. In 1166 prominence was given to a jury of accusation or presentment. In every shire twelve men from each hundred and four men from each vill were to swear that they would make true answer to the question whether any man was reputed to have been guilty of murder, robbery, larceny or harbouring criminals since the king's coronation. Further refinements were made later; the crimes of forgery and arson were added to the list. The accused had at this stage to go to the ordeal. Inquests were to be made before the itinerant justices. Practice surely did not always live up to the smooth declaration of the lawyers, but by the end of the Angevin period standard processes of peace-keeping involving itinerant justices, shire courts, juries and original writs were common to the whole of the English community.

Tendencies towards unity and uniformity were brought together in the reign of King John. No medieval English king has left a worse reputation, and those who base their history on chronicles can readily see why. Men were ready to believe him guilty of murdering his nephew, starving to death political prisoners and generally behaving as a tyrant, an affront to church and secular alike. From this angle King John contributed mightily to the national myth. He became the archetypal wicked uncle, faithless brother, odious tyrant, the perfect foil in later historical fiction to good King Richard and Robin Hood. Historians who base their analysis on administrative records have better things to say of him. He was undoubtedly energetic, and his apparent rapacity and cupidity can to some measure be explained by the sheer economic pressure of an inflationary age. Even so, the bare political sequence of the loss of Normandy and most of the Continental possessions, followed by a quarrel with the church that left England under interdict from the pope, puts heavy weight on the negative balance. Attempts to reclaim the French lands were expensive failures. Submission to the pope, reducing the kingdom to the status of a papal fief, proved the only way of resolving temporarily the political crisis. Massive discontent forced the issue of Magna Carta, and another element in the national myth was born. It is all very well to say that it was chance that made Magna Carta important: the death of John from his surfeit of peaches and new wine in 1216, the need to buttress the authority of a nine-year-old minor in the person of his son, Henry III. And it is true that the charter was in one sense a failure. Its attempt to limit permanently the actions of a king who acted contrary to law was unworkable and was omitted from the reissues, including, of course, from what became the authoritative reissue of 1225. Nevertheless, as a statement of the rule of law it caught the imagination of later generations, was invoked whenever personal or public rights seemed infringed by royal authority, and by the end of the thirteenth century was enrolled as the first statute of the realm.

In detail, the clauses of Magna Carta provide a rich insight into the society of the day. The modern reader is surprised initially at the concern shown over the incidents of feudal society: the attempts to regulate fair payment of reliefs on entering inheritance and to safeguard widows, marriage rights of daughters, wardship and the treatment of minors. Like so many medieval documents, it is something of a hotchpotch, and important observations on what amount to peace settlements in Wales and Scotland sit uneasily with the assertion of rights over fish weirs in the Thames. Things are not always what they seem. The charter opens with a splendid statement that the *anglicana ecclesia* shall be free, but such freedom in 1215 meant freedom to be under the papacy, and true concern lay with control of elections and rights over finance. The conservative nature of the document comes out strongly in its insistence that ordinary lawsuits should not follow the royal court on its wanderings but be held at a fixed place. The possessory assizes (and *novel disseisin* is given prior place) were to be held in their proper shire court. Itinerant justices were to hold their courts, with four knights elected by the shire, four times a year. Some safeguard was built in to feudal courts, but the overwhelming concern of Magna Carta was to see that royal justice was well conducted and abuse removed. It was in that sense an elaborate commentary at a fixed moment in time on the ideals embodied in the coronation charter of Henry I and ultimately on the coronation oath itself.

Two clauses stand out, not only for their immediate impact as resistance to abuse, but as inspiration to the future and, again, as part of the general urge towards good government that bound the community together. Clause 39 of Magna Carta stated that no free man should be seized or imprisoned or stripped of his rights or possessions or outlawed or exiled, or deprived of his standing in any other way, nor would the king proceed against him with force, or send others to do so, except by the lawful judgment of his peers or by the law of the land. Clause 40 was briefer and yet more potent. The king pledged himself that to no one would he sell, deny or delay justice. Great debate is possible over the practical force of these statements, the limitations of the definition of 'free man', the possibility that judgment of peers is an adjunct to 'law of the land' rather than an alternative. It seems perverse, however, not to recognize here an affirmation of the basic principle of the rule of law, a recognition that in mature medieval political theory a legitimate king was one who ruled justly according to the law. There is substantial as well as symbolic strength in Magna Carta which enabled later generations to read it as a cornerstone of English liberties, the 'Bible of the English Constitution'.

CHAPTER 7

Henry III (1216–72):
English kingship and baronial unrest

Henry III was born on 1 October 1207, the son of King John and Isabella of Angoulême. He succeeded his father in October 1216, achieved a limited personal majority in 1223 and a full majority in January 1227. Isabella, a passionate and ambitious woman, returned to Angoulême after John's death and married Hugh, count of Lusignan, in conditions of some scandal; she herself had been betrothed at an earlier stage to Hugh's father, and plans had been made for a marriage between Hugh and Joan, her and John's own daughter! The ambitions and cupidity of the Lusignans, offspring of this new marriage, were to cause great trouble to their half-brother Henry III in the late 1240s and 1250s.

Henry's reign proved to be longer than that of any other monarch till the reign of Victoria, and yet it is curious how little an impact he made on the national legend. He was no great soldier, but neither was he a coward nor a non-combatant. In 1250 he took the cross and at that stage presumably intended to go on crusade. Part of his failure to achieve reputation must be put down to the simple fact that he was surrounded by men more powerful in character than he: William Marshall and Stephen Langton in his earlier days, to some extent his brother Richard of Cornwall (1209–72; king of the Romans from 1257), Simon de Montfort, and his own son Edward (1239–1307) in his later years. His royal cousin, Louis IX of France, St Louis (1226–70), was the dominant personality of the Anglo-French world, and Henry, though not completely subservient and quite capable of fighting for English or Gascon interests against the French king, normally deferred to the personal, political and spiritual prestige of St Louis. Henry was also unfortunate in his historians. The contemporary who knew him best was the conservative and crotchety Matthew Paris of St Albans, and Henry was at times the target for what can only be called the sheer bitchiness of the monastic historian. The king's undoubted religious sense was dismissed as subservience to the pope; the failure of a Gascon expedition was attributed to his poor qualities as a soldier; legitimate and necessary taxation was condemned as plunder and extortion, especially harmful to the English church; friendship and amiability were twisted into fondness for flattery and favouritism. When the king planned to go on crusade Matthew Paris delivered this admonition:

> Would that the lord king of the English and his brother Earl Richard and other crusading princes intent on obtaining filthy lucre would weigh these things in the scales of reason. For though the act of holy pilgrimage is agreed to be pious, yet travelling expenses acquired dishonourably defile the performance of the pious deed.

The poor man could not win. It is true, as Richard Vaughan, his modern biographer, has pointed out, that Matthew Paris' strictures should be read as a characteristically English hatred of authority; he disapproved strongly of all government except the hanging of thieves. Matthew Paris himself died in 1259, as the constitutional struggles leading to the Barons' War reached a peak; this was just as well for Henry's reputation, which would certainly have been further blackened if Paris had had his say on the events of 1259–65. Modern historians are beginning to redress the balance, and Sir Maurice Powicke, who thought of Henry as 'a decent man, a man to be reckoned with', reminded us that he left England 'more prosperous, more united, more peaceful, more beautiful, than it was when he was a child'.

There is certainly full justification for suggesting an increase in prosperity, as anyone who has studied the urban, ecclesiastical and architectural history of the reign will readily agree. Indeed, wealth and complexity are the two dominant impressions that the surviving evidence gives to the student of thirteenth-century England as a whole, especially perhaps to the student of the middle years and

143

third quarter of the century. The outer skin of events is rich enough, with Magna Carta, the Marshall family, the great justiciar Hubert de Burgh, French, Poitevin and Lusignan influence, Simon de Montfort and the Baronial War; but the inner administrative and financial core is even richer.

Angevin tendencies to despotism were checked by the revolt of 1215. Magna Carta, reissued in 1216 and 1217 with major modifications, and again in final accepted form in 1225, remained a symbol of the rule of law throughout the century and far beyond. Angevin skill in administration was not checked, however, and the thirteenth century proved to be a great bureaucratic age. Lawyers, professional justices and administrators came steadily to replace bishops and soldiers as the chief agents of government. The century was fecund in the growth of institutions and in record-keeping. Still interlocked and complex, the Chancery and the Exchequer constituted the great offices of state, powerful, if constrained to some extent by their own traditions and precedents. The royal household proliferated in institutional creations – some, such as the Chamber and the Wardrobe, to assume long-lasting life, others to enjoy temporary existence only. Record-keeping became a fine art, and the massive bulk of Pipe Rolls, Close Rolls and Patent Rolls, each with its separate progeny as business increased in volume, remain a testimony to the force of royal literate administration and also a storehouse for the historian. Fine, Memoranda and Originalia Rolls continued to be issued from Chancery. Wardrobe accounts, Receipt Rolls and Issue Rolls form basic sources and supplements to the Pipe Rolls for our knowledge of thirteenth-century finance.

Legal records were kept more systematically as court procedures helped to clarify the separateness of the function of the great central law courts, the King's Bench and Common Pleas. Original writs multiplied. As we shall see later, the Hundred Rolls, consequent upon a great inquest held in 1274–5 by Edward I, record the tangled network of royal and private jurisdictions that had flourished in his father's reign. By the end of the century regular Year Books were appearing, recording the principal cases of interest heard in the law courts at Westminster and creating a set of easily available known precedents for a later generation of lawyers. The survival of records

144

from a few county and franchisal courts and from many manorial courts indicates how the need for a written statement of legal decisions and, *a fortiori*, of legal precedent was felt deep in society. Magna Carta retained special prestige as a symbol, as well as in substance, and was slowly accepted as an equivalent of written law, Statute Law. At a great council that met at Merton in January 1236 Henry III issued a statute that declared law over a whole range of social matters, safeguarding widows and minors, protecting successful litigants against further discussion, and allowing lords to enclose common pastures provided that the customary rights of the tenants were respected. The settlement after the civil war was embodied in the Statute of Marlborough (1267). England already, even before the spate of central activity on the part of Edward I and his lawyers, was well on the way to the creation of a body of precise written law. Distinction between statutes and ordinances was still a matter for the future, but no comment on the inner history of the reign of Henry III would be satisfactory that failed to take into account the intense legal activity, theoretical as well as practical, that characterized the intellectual life of the so-called 'Age of Bracton'.

Bracton himself was from 1245 a royal judge who had a busy career in practical law on the King's Bench, who also worked as a justice in the south-western shires, and who, in the last years of his life (d. 1268), served on a commission that inquired into the state of the disinherited after the Montfort rebellion. His fame rests on his great treatise *De Legibus et Consuetudinibus Angliæ*, written in the 1250s. His method of analysis and classification owed much to the revival of Roman Law, but the substance of his treatise was peculiarly English, with the emphasis on case law and precedent. At the constitutional level, he did not follow the arbitrary principles found in Justinian's Code, but held that the king was under law. In a famous dictum, deeply influential on English legal and political thought in the following generations, he stated that 'the king ought not to be under man but under God and the law, because the law made the king'. These were fine words, but not much help in the critical situation that arose in 1258, when the king appeared to be acting against the law. Nevertheless, the presence of one of the most influential legal thinkers of his age in the courts of King Henry illustrates the sophisticated and complex level of the English community.

From the point of view of the economic historian, administrative and legal development of the type experienced between 1216 and 1258 is best interpreted as a reflection of increased prosperity. This is not always so. In ancient empires bureaucracies could flourish temporarily as economies crumbled, but the English example, based as it was on an economy still predominantly agrarian, was a very different case. Increased efficiency in the handling of arable land had been the basic cause of the increase in population in the twelfth century, but now other factors were beginning to apply. Trade became more regular and intense both at the inter-regional and internal levels. Fairs and markets were better regulated, and from early in the reign of Henry III there was a tendency for markets to be moved from Sundays to weekdays, and from churchyards to secular sites. There was a steady proliferation of towns, and urban life became more orderly and better regulated.

London, as always, showed clearest signs of moving into a new world. Its commune had won its place in the struggles of the reign of King John, so that it started the new reign as a self-governing city with a good tradition of unity behind it. Its population grew, probably doubling in the course of the century to a figure of 40,000 or so. Its boundaries also grew, spreading out particularly over the western suburbs. There was a substantial influx of settlers, traders and craftsmen, from the Home Counties and East Anglia in great number, but also from elsewhere in Britain, even from the north and from Scotland. Settlement from Europe was also far from negligible, mostly in specialized groups connected with finance and long-distance trade in wood, wine, metals, spices and leather. London was the attractive entrepôt at the edges of European commerce, a fit target for the enterprising from the Flemish and Italian connection, for German merchants from the Rhineland, and for Gascon merchants busy in the wine trade. The main routes were still by land, with Paris and Bruges the two principal centres from which merchants made their link with London, and it was not until the reign of Henry's son Edward that we can be sure that Mediterranean galleys from Italian ports and Majorca were beginning to open up the sea-route to the north that was to enrich the commercial life of Europe in the late Middle Ages. Matthew Paris in 1255 complained that London was overflowing with Poitevins, Provençals and Italians. Cahorsin moneylenders were notorious. Scandinavian and Spanish traders knew the familiar route to the metropolis on the Thames. Even so, political power in what was rapidly developing into a true capital city rested for the most part in the hands of a well-established group of patrician families, drawing their strength from landed possessions in London and the neighbouring shires, and at times taking mayoral office: the Rengers, the Bukerels, the FitzAilwins, the Hadestoks, the de Basings and de Gisors.

One of the reasons for this concentration of burghal power was the proximity of the centre of royal government at Westminster and the resulting trade in all matters affecting the royal household, in its public as well as private attributes. The principal figure in the city was the mayor, who led great processions at the main ecclesiastical feasts, representing the city and often the shires of Middlesex and Essex as well. On 23 October the new mayor would preside over one of the most colourful events in the London year, leading a procession in honour of Bishop William, who had safeguarded civic rights at the time of the Norman Conquest, and paying special homage to the house of the martyred Thomas Becket, regarded by all Londoners as one of their number. The mayor was drawn from the group of wealthy aldermen who usually held office for life. Wool-traders, vintners, goldsmiths, drapers, pepperers and mercers were among the most prosperous of traders, but organized groups of craftsmen were also busy and active in the life of the city.

The wealth generated in London had much to contribute to the feeling of unity in the nation, but there was also much turbulence, violence and poverty. In 1257 the aldermen claimed that many had not goods to the value of one of the king's new golden pennies, and in the following year there was famine on a scale that shook the self-confidence of the whole community. The Provisions of Oxford, enacted by the baronial council in the summer of 1258, made specific mention of the need to reform the state of the city of London, and of all the other cities of the king, which had gone to poverty and ruin on account of tallages and other oppressions, though harsh politics as much as economic reality determined the form of this enactment.

Where London led, other cities and boroughs quickly followed. Simon de Montfort, in his efforts to establish peace during the winter of 1264–5, summoned to his parliament in the January, by direct writ to the citizens of York, Lincoln and all the other boroughs, two of the most prudent, law-worthy and honourable citizens or burgesses. London and the Cinque Ports were treated separately, and the writ of summons for Sandwich enjoins the barons and bailiffs of the port to send four of the more lawful and prudent men to treat with the king and magistrates, and to give counsel. This was the first parliament to which borough representatives were called, a taste of things to come, and also an indication of the way in which settled urban communities were providing a context for a sense of community within the realm of England. Urban archaeology is still in a relatively early stage of development, but already it is beginning to illuminate some of the problems. Evidence from Southampton is particularly helpful. The loss of Normandy made no impact on the course of prosperity in that bustling seaport, and the massive stone houses of the prosperous burgesses reveal part of the story of thirteenth-century conditions; glazed windows appear in some of the greater town houses. Stone-built cesspits tell of better attention paid to hygiene. Analysis of pollen and plant-seed show a marked improvement in quality and variety of diet, and there is evidence for a specialization of butchery, with a greater demand for veal and sucking-pig and many different kinds of poultry and wildfowl.

Urban communities shared common problems, adopted similar customs and paid common dues to the crown or to the seignorial lord. There was great variety in size and importance. Some, such as York, Norwich, Chester and Bristol, grew into very substantial regional capitals. Perhaps the best example of urban vitality in the reign of Henry III comes from a slightly unexpected and, one might argue, special quarter: the town of Salisbury. It has been estimated that over one hundred new towns were founded in England between 1066 and 1300, but no foundation was more spectacular and significant than that of Salisbury. The old town, 'Old Sarum', was well-established from Roman days and beyond, overlooking the east bank of the river Avon, about two miles from the site on the plain chosen for the foundation of the new thirteenth-century town. Its dramatic, compressed situation on a hill-top had served it well as a royal stronghold, with moneyers, a mint and a market. There were disadvantages, however. Old Sarum was also the diocesan head-quarters with a great cathedral of an important bishopric, and tensions between the chapter and the garrison were inevitable, reaching crisis point in the second decade of the thirteenth century. In 1217 a petition was made, at a time when the influence of papal legates was at its maximum, for the cathedral to be moved to a valley site on the Avon at a point that provided topographically an ideal focus for routes leading along the five principal river valleys of South Wiltshire. The petition was granted and the money found for the building of what is still one of the glories of European architecture: Salisbury cathedral, an almost perfect example of the Early English Gothic style. The altars of the Trinity Chapel were consecrated in 1225, and the main structure of the huge church was almost complete by the end of Henry's reign, with of course the exception of the central tower and spire, a supreme achievement of the middle years of the fourteenth century.

From the beginning the economic and social implications of the move were well understood, and the wealth and activity connected with the building of the cathedral stimulated urban growth. Licences for a market and fair were granted almost *ab initio*; and in 1224 the market was licensed for the whole year. An episcopal charter in 1225 set up what was called the free city of New Salisbury, to be followed two years later by a royal charter. Letters were sent in the name of the king to nine sheriffs and to twenty-seven towns, including Bristol and Exeter, to inform them of the grant. Freedom of toll in demesne and assimilation of customs and liberties to those of Winchester formed the principal buttresses of townsmen's rights, and the new town quickly attracted enterprising new settlers, to the detriment and partial ruin of Old Sarum and, indeed, of Wilton. The building of a great stone bridge of ten arches over the Avon in 1244, leading traffic to the south, proved a further important stimulus to growth. Exploitation of the advantages of the low-lying site seems to have been well-controlled: broad streets, open water-channels, and many bridges were characteristic. At the same time growth was rapid and based on the economic realities of agrarian, sheep-rearing, wool-providing activity as much as on administrative and ecclesiastical pressures. There is some evidence for the existence of standard plots, but even more of entrepreneurial vagaries in the size and shape of urban holdings. Administratively, the town was divided into four aldermanries, called wards. By the end of Henry III's reign new permanent parishes were established. St Nicholas' Hospital was reformed in the 1230s. Both Franciscan and Dominican friars settled in Salisbury, and academic vitality was shown by the presence of twenty scholars in 1262 at the College de Vaux. Salisbury, with its great cathedral and new town, provides an outstanding – though not the only – example of the way in which the English communities were settling to permanent and relatively prosperous communal life in the middle years of the thirteenth century.

Temptation to treat urban growth in isolation is great, but must be resisted. For the mass of the population, still something in the order of nine-tenths, growing food or rearing cattle, sheep or other domestic animals was the prime economic motive in life. There was such variety within that bland framework from region to region, district to district, manor to manor, that all generalizations are to some extent suspect. As always, the basic difference between the harsher uplands of the north and west, and the gentler lands of chalk and limestone, sandstone and clay of the south and east imposed a major contrast in way of life on the inhabitants of England. The historian has to rely on two principal sources for information: written evidence and archaeological findings. Written records are extensive but inevitably weighted in favour of the large estates, where record-keeping and even reflection on the theory of farming could be indulged in. Thirteenth-century England is surprisingly rich in the production of treatises on husbandry; all lived near the soil. The greatest scholar of the age, Robert Grosseteste, bishop of Lincoln (1235–53), could find time to instruct Hawise de Quincy, countess of Lincoln, on the management of estates, advising her on the yields she should expect from her corn-growing lands. The archaeologist, asking increasingly refined questions about manorial complexes, field systems and peasants' houses, grows closer again to reality, but deserted villages demand time, money and energy if they are to yield their secrets, and the very continuity of so much English village life leaves medieval evidence hard to find. Even so, an agreed general picture that may be near the truth is beginning to emerge.

The high inflation of 1180–1220 had caused something of a revolution in rural life. Slavery disappeared as a significant element, but the weight of labour service increased as landlords found it in their interest to insist on ancient rights and dues, and as peasants found themselves more dependent on the forces of a wider market, particularly in areas where their standard of living and expectations improved. Some increase in the use of three-field systems in place of two-field systems occurred, though the extent and significance of such change is still a matter for debate. Technical improvements – the use of windmills for power and better awareness of means of preserving soil fertility – made formidable impact in some favoured areas. The revival of high farming, often stimulated by ecclesiastical landlords, led to a general increase in prosperity in arable and sheep farming, notably where farming merged into the textile industries, the provision of wool and cloth. Cistercian mastery of sheep-rearing techniques extended the range of prosperity to upland regions. As always, such general increase was not evenly shared. Some regions benefited more than others, and by and large the lords of greater and medium-sized estates benefited most. They could control the advantages that came from wider marketing and urban development; and it is against this background that the political and social importance of the resident knights of the shire should be read. Archaeologists have shown that a great number of our moated sites had their origins in the thirteenth century; the fact that they are sometimes built on marginal land indicates the nature of agrarian expansion, directed by lords who could command the sort of labour capable of putting up substantial houses protected by water defences. These moats or water defences were there probably to safeguard stock rather than to serve as military defence against hostile forces, and, indeed, the spread of moated sites later in the Middle Ages is best explained in terms of their importance as status symbols, rather than as institutions with a functional purpose. But visually and socially they hint again at the widespread consolidation of local authority in the hands of knights of the shire.

As for the lesser men, the archaeologist helps with his insistence that the thirteenth century experienced a breakthrough in the use of stone for peasants' houses. This was not universal, and in some areas timber building remained normal throughout the Middle Ages. But where stone was readily available, in parts of the south-west and along the chalk and limestone belts from the south coast to deep into Yorkshire, it became more common to use stone and flint for the walling or partial walling of the houses of lesser men. Not all could afford such; wages appear to have remained stable during a period of steadily rising prices. Lawyers, acting as social theorists, extolled the continuity of peasant holdings within families, but partible inheritance and a rising population swelled the number of landless peasants. In such a context it seems likely that the prosperity suggested by more substantial building applied principally to those who could benefit most from the market, that is to say the manorial officers, reeves and bailiffs, the laymen who helped administer church lands, and a class of the more prosperous families from whom such officers would be mostly drawn. It is all well and good to talk of uniform villeinage, but that was an ill-formed legal concept. Social distinctions within the peasantry intensified in the thirteenth century as the economy itself became more sophisticated.

A measure of the degree of sophistication within the economy can be found in the currency; and one sure link between town and countryside can be well appreciated when we look at the state of the coinage. The introduction of the short-cross coinage in 1180 had not been a great success. Coins inscribed *Henricus Rex* continued to be struck during the reigns of Richard and John, and it takes considerable numismatic skill to be able to place such coins chronologically right through to the 1240s. London was the most important centre and the home of a hierarchy of officers headed by a master, a royal appointment, and a warden, who had special responsibility for collecting dues that should rightly go to the king. There was also an assay master who had to check the fineness and quality of the coins, and a *cuneator*, or die-master, who superintended the engravers of dies and saw to their circulation from London to other mints. Grave dissatisfaction was felt and expressed at the serious debasement of the coins, silver pennies and half pennies, mostly by clipping, a practice attributed by public opinion to Jews, Flemings or Cahorsins – all those, in other words, actively involved in transactions that demanded financial expertise of a relatively advanced nature. In 1247 a massive reform was undertaken, to all appearance under the inspiration of, and certainly to the immense financial profit of, the king's brother Richard, earl of Cornwall. The old coins were called in, and new coins of good quality issued from November 1247. Provision was made for seventeen local mints, each of which was to have in theory at least four moneyers, four keepers of the dies, two assayers and a clerk.

On 11 March 1248 we have our first record of the trial of the pyx, by which the fineness of the new coins was tested. The cross on the reverse of the coin was lengthened, possibly to make clipping more difficult, and the royal inscription on the obverse was altered to include an abbreviation of *tercius*, Henry the '*third*'. Circulation of foreign money, especially Scottish, was expressly forbidden. The recoinage was successful, a sensible, conservative and efficient measure typical of Richard of Cornwall himself, who proceeded over the following twelve years or so to draw a substantial fortune from his rights in the venture.

Reform of the silver penny coinage provided confidence in the basic economy, though larger transactions depended on movement of bullion assessed in the units of accounts, pounds and marks. In 1257 a further development took place, aesthetically pleasing, though of little immediate practical significance. An attempt was made to introduce a gold penny, initially at a ratio of twenty to one over the silver. It was not a great success, and seems to have been withdrawn from circulation towards the end of the reign. There was no further issue of gold until January 1344, but the issue of 1257 shows that there were men of influence in England well aware of European developments. After nearly six centuries during which Western Europe had relied on the equivalent of their silver penny as the normal coin, Florence took the lead in 1252 in striking the gold florin. The end of the so-called denarial economy was in sight, and

England showed itself ready poised to play a modest part in the currency changes of the age.

Powerful economic and social forces were therefore helping to mould the English nation into a common awareness of its heritage and individuality. Yet the king, the court, the aristocracy, the high churchmen were still overwhelmingly French in language, culture and social habit. It was taken as unusual and worthy of comment that Richard of Cornwall, the king's brother, was fluent in English; and part of his success in winning over the Rhineland to support his candidature as king of the Romans and potential emperor (1257–72) was ascribed to his knowledge of English, since it sounded so like the German tongue. But French was used increasingly in official business, even at the expense of Latin. During the baronial revolt of the late 1250s the agreement made between the king and the barons, known as the Provisions of Oxford (June–July 1258), was made in French (except for the opening clause in Latin), though it is of considerable interest to note that Henry III declared both in French and in English, in his letters patent to the shires, his acceptance on 18 October 1258 of the provisions that had been forced on him in the Oxford parliament. French came, in fact, to dominate legal records and continued to do so well into the later Middle Ages. English, of course, continued to be used in pleading and giving evidence in lower courts, but record-keeping was quite another matter.

In the literary world also there was an apparent dominance of Latin and French. Yet for the student of English literature, though there are no great names, the thirteenth century is not without interest and compensations. The spread of Romance, the use of rhyme, increasing familiarity with the legends and history of Troy, of Greece, of Arthur and the Matter of Britain, of Charlemagne, had immense impact on the vernacular, a high proportion of it by oral transmission. The basic rule still persisted, however: an educated man spoke and wrote French or Latin; a scholar wrote Latin; English remained predominantly the language of the marketplace and of lesser men and women.

In spite of class divisions, dramatically exemplified in linguistic habits, a sense of nationhood grew and flourished in the course of the thirteenth century. How did this come about? The basic political patterns of the century undoubtedly helped in both church and state. The process was continuous, and yet differences in emphasis coincide with the differences in personality of the rulers Henry III and Edward I. Under Henry III the sense of community grows in opposition, from underneath. Edward I, in personality and political activity, was more positive and was able to harness the sense of communal identity to create a strong monarchy of England.

Something has already been said of the administrative and governmental progress made during the reign of Henry III. Politically, the atmosphere was much more troubled. Henry was only nine years old when his father died in 1216, but a strong regency guided the monarchy during the first decade of the reign, dominated by the personalities of William Marshall (d. 1218), Archbishop Stephen Langton (d. 1228) and, initially, by the papal legates. The powerful justiciar Hubert de Burgh carried the monarchy through the turbulent end of the minority, when the young king, acting true to type of most men in such situations, asserted himself by engaging in half-hearted and fruitless campaigns in Brittany and Wales. He brought back into favour the old ministerial family that had owed so much to John, Peter des Roches, bishop of Winchester, and his nephew, Peter des Rivaux. Between them they forced the retirement of de Burgh in 1232, and for the following quarter of a century Henry III, the most cultured of the Angevins, exercised a personal rule that was fitfully autocratic, and which ended substantially in failure and civil war. Nevertheless, it was a period of great consequence in the moulding of the English nation.

There were two focal points for political discontent, both of them partly the product of Henry's own character – the question of foreign favourites and the question of papal authority over the English church. The English baronage had moved far towards acquiring an insular identity of their own, and the intrusion of fresh groups of Frenchmen, particularly of Frenchmen from south of the Loire, from Poitou and Lusignan, into positions of favour and influence roused much envy. Oddly enough, it was one of the chief newcomers, Simon de Montfort, who finally took the lead against his brother-in-law, the English king. In August 1231 the young Simon succeeded in winning recognition of his family claim to the earldom of Leicester. In January 1238 he married Eleanor, the king's sister, in conditions of some scandal (she had taken a vow of chastity). The crusading son of a most famous crusading father, he had aspirations to yet higher things. He governed Gascony vigorously in the king's name from 1248 to 1252, but increasingly fell out with his brother-in-law in the 1250s and became progressively identified with the English baronial interest. In 1258 he was one of a group of prominent men protesting at what they saw as the extravagance and misgovernment of the king. In the July of that year, while they were both sheltering from a thunderstorm, Henry III is said to have confessed to Simon that much as he feared lightning, he feared the earl even more. Montfort was no political genius, and it was not until 1263 that he emerged as the unquestioned leader of a baronial party; but his sheer force of personality, military skill and capacity for violence made him a figure larger than life. He was conventionally pious, close to Bishop Grosseteste of Lincoln and his successors among the clerical hierarchy. His insistence after 1263 on principles of reform left him with a good reputation among churchmen, the middle rank of men in the countryside and many townsmen, notably Londoners. His victory at Lewes in 1264 and the savage reversal of defeat and death at Evesham in the following year made him ripe material for the chronicler and the moralists. Miracles were reported at his tomb soon after his death. Clerical friends of a later generation perpetuated the myth of the reforming earl, and later generations looked to him as the father of Parliament. The symbolic afterlife of de Montfort is as significant in the making of the nation as the career itself.

In many respects Simon de Montfort's career provides a contrast and counterpoint to that of his other brother-in-law, Richard, younger brother of Henry III. Richard was made earl of Cornwall in 1227, acquired the great fiefs of Berkhamsted and Wallingford, and by his marriage in 1231 to Isabella (d. 1240), heiress to much of the wealth of the Marshall family, became one of the natural leaders of the insular interest. Heir presumptive to the English throne until the birth of Edward in 1239, Richard seems, however, by inclination and nature to have filled the role of mediator, and from 1240, in part as a consequence of his later marriages to Sanchia of Provence (1242) and Beatrice of Falkenburg (1269), looked for fulfilment of wider ambitions elsewhere. Until 1243 he aimed to achieve a principality in the South of France, and in the 1250s aspired with some success to the imperial throne. He was never crowned emperor, but he was recognized as, and crowned, king of the Romans (1257–72) and enjoyed the dignity, if not the authority over parts of Germany, notably the Rhineland, that went with that rank. These great men, Simon de Montfort and Richard of Cornwall, are interesting in their potentiality for leadership in times of political crisis. Even more interesting is the groundswell of baronial resentment at the wealth and apparent power – much exaggerated – acquired by, for example, the queen's kinsfolk from Savoy or the Lusignans.

The papal question was more intricate. Henry III was a deeply religious man; Matthew Paris tells how, when a phial of the Lord's blood arrived from the Holy Land in 1247, the king himself, humbly dressed, led our first recorded Corpus Christi procession on foot from St Paul's to Westminster. He owed much to the wisdom and good sense of the papal legates in the early years of the minority. But the papacy itself was passing through a period of great financial difficulty. It needed money and support for political reasons, in prosecuting its quarrel with the Hohenstaufen emperor Frederick II (1212–50), and also for its own internal reasons as it developed its bureaucracy in the interests of papal monarchy. At the very moment when royal demands were growing great on the English church, so now too did papal demands, to all appearance with the support of the English crown. The depth of feeling roused is best studied in the career of the greatest English churchman of the day, Grosseteste, bishop of Lincoln (1235-53). Scientist and theologian, he twice visited Rome, in 1245 and in 1250, to protest against papal provision of unsuitable men to spiritual office in England and, on his second visit, to widen his brief into an impassioned yet reasoned attack on the papacy and the curia. He even brought himself to the point where he talked of the perversion of Christ's representative on earth acting contrary to Christ in his principal operations. His attack was ineffective. He retained personally full orthodoxy of belief, though his views were later taken up zealously by Wycliffe. But early in 1251, when the debate at Rome was fresh in his mind and when his friend Simon de Montfort was under attack for his oppressive rule in Gascony, Grosseteste sent to Simon part of his brief, in which he had expounded his views of the distinctions between just rule and tyranny. Matthew Paris, regularly vociferous against foreigners and papal demands, made much of this element of opposition in Grosseteste's character when he summed up, in moving and eloquent prose, the bishop's virtues:

> an open reprover of pope and king, a critic of prelates, a corrector of monks, a director of priests, a preacher to the people, a sustainer of scholars, a diligent student of Scripture, a hammer and despiser of the Romans; hospitable, liberal, urbane, cheerful, affable in his hall; devout, tearful, contrite in church; diligent, grave, untiring in his episcopal duties.

The full crisis in English relations with the papacy developed soon after the death of Grosseteste. The emperor Frederick II had died in 1250, and his son and heir, Conrad IV, in 1254. The papacy was anxious to free Sicily from Hohenstaufen influence, and found in Henry III a willing though injudicious ally. In 1254 Henry agreed to accept the crown of Sicily on behalf of his second son, Edmund. He also agreed to pay a massive sum in redemption of papal debt, an ill-advised step that forced the opposition to unite in England and so precipitated the constitutional crisis of 1258. Yet it would be a distortion to portray Henry III simply as a Gallophile facing a steadily mounting nationalistic opposition to extravagant Continental schemes. He was probably more aware than any king since the Norman Conquest of the solidity of his English inheritance. Much of his best aesthetic and spiritual ardour, to say nothing of his financial resources, was poured into the rebuilding of Westminster Abbey. He felt an accord with Edward the Confessor, holding Edward personally (and therefore by implication the line of continuity with Anglo-Saxon kings) in special veneration. His two eldest sons were called Edward and Edmund. Foreign favourites, respect for the papacy and commitment to his Angevin and French ancestry did not blind him to his English heritage. His attempts to regain some of his lost Angevin lands ended in disaster or fiasco. Very sensibly, he reached an agreement with his kinsman Louis IX of France that was given final legal shape as late as 1259 by the Treaty of Paris, under the terms of which Henry promised homage and fealty for Gascony and Aquitaine as a peer of France, while renouncing all claim to other lands, even to the ancestral fiefs of Anjou and Normandy. In both England and France the centripetal force inherent in feudalism was helping to create national monarchies in their respective communities.

The true testing time for the English monarchy came in the long-drawn-out struggle, from 1258 to 1265, between the king and his baronage. Royal weakness lay in the financial field. The king could not live on his own and, as his overseas commitments grew, he was forced to summon a great council to Oxford in the summer of 1258, which virtually substituted rule by a council of fifteen for the curial government of the period of personal rule. The attempt to run a monarchy without a king was not successful. Splits appeared within the baronage, and the political situation slowly hardened out into a royal party, headed by the Lord Edward, the king's son, and a baronial party, led by Simon de Montfort and the new young earl of Gloucester, Gilbert de Clare, who succeeded his father in July 1262. King Louis was called upon to arbitrate and, by the Mise of Amiens in January 1264, found in favour of the king. Civil war broke out, and de Montfort won the battle of Lewes, 14 May 1264, capturing the king and Richard of Cornwall, and forcing Edward and his cousin Henry of Almain to accept a truce and to surrender themselves as hostages.

For the best part of a twelvemonth, Montfort was effective ruler of England. He reconstituted a baronial council, this time of nine members, and summoned assemblies, the Montfort 'parliaments', to secure a wide basis of support. At his second parliament, in January 1265, burgesses from the boroughs joined knights of the shire to give counsel in matters concerning the community of the realm, including, it would seem, the liberation of Prince Edward. A precedent was set, which his chief opponent, Prince Edward himself, was later to use to advantage. Meanwhile, in late May 1265

Edward, after a period of relatively comfortable house arrest in the company of his father and Simon, escaped to join forces with the young earl of Gloucester, newly estranged from the Montfort cause. The royalist party won a crushing victory at Evesham on 4 August 1265, killing Montfort and his key supporters, and mutilating his body.

In contrast to the savagery on the field, there was relatively little vindictiveness in the settlement that followed. The class interests, and indeed the family interests, of the ruling group as a whole were enough to mitigate the effects of personal hatreds; and a general prosperity helped to temper the severity of political rivalries. By the Dictum of Kenilworth, October 1266, those who surrendered after Evesham were treated as rebels. The integrity of the kingdom was assured and there was to be no more playing with the idea of legitimate private warfare. The rebels who survived recovered their lands and the king's favour on payment of a heavy fine, some of which was still being paid deep into Edward's reign. The best features of baronial plans for legal reform were incorporated into the Statute of Marlborough, 1267. Prince Edward assumed a dominant role in council and succeeded his father in 1272 without difficulty, even though he was in the Holy Land on crusade at the moment of succession. The constitutional crisis, by a quirk of fortune, left the monarchy strengthened and in the capable hands of an experienced thirty-two-year-old ruler of great prestige and still greater potential.

CHAPTER 8

Edward I and the English monarchy

Matthew Paris, firm-minded even when wrong, knew Edward in his younger days and saw a streak of cruelty in him that boded ill for the future. Fortunately for England, Matthew Paris was mistaken. As Michael Prestwich has shown in a recent biography of Edward I (on which the following paragraph relies heavily), there were some who accused the Lord Edward of duplicity during the Barons' War and talked of the virtues and vices of the panther or the leopard. But he was not a cruel man; by the time of his death the favoured analogy was with the valour and strength of the lion. Edward was a man of courage, winning the respect of men he led in war, on crusade, at tournaments or in the hunting field. He killed with his own hands the assassin who attacked him at Acre with a poisoned dagger, and stories of his recovery (later legend had Eleanor, his wife, herself sucking the wound) stress his courage in facing medical treatment and primitive surgery. On his way home from crusade in 1273 he took part in a tournament at Châlons which degenerated into a brawl. He emerged from it as victor thanks to his own superior physical strength, dragging his chief opponent, Count Peter, from his saddle and forcing him to the ground. He could be rash and headstrong: during the siege of Stirling in 1304 – he was still active in his sixties – he exposed himself unnecessarily to danger and had his horse felled under him, a crossbow shaft lodged in the saddle. His piety was conventional and unsophisticated, which did not stop him from quarrelling violently with his archbishop, Robert of Winchelsey, and with other bishops when he felt royal interests were threatened. He was a good family man, devoted to his first wife Eleanor of Castile, by whom he had at least fourteen children. She died in 1290 when they were on a hunting trip together at Harby

(Notts), and her body was taken for burial to Westminster. Edward had the great Eleanor crosses built at each of the places where her body rested on its journey south. Three still survive, at Geddington, Hardingstone and Waltham Cross, and replicas have been built at other points, notably Charing Cross in London. Edward also seems to have been happy with, and faithful to his young second wife Margaret of France, whom he married in 1299, although complaints were made of her extravagance. A large man, over six foot in height, he was strong and given to occasional outbursts of temper. A famous story tells how on one occasion he hurled his daughter's coronet into the fire, but then later paid for it to be restored. He was not insensitive to the arts and architecture, and modern attribution of much of the painted chamber at Westminster to his reign and the 1290s, rather than to his father's in the 1260s, makes good sense. He enjoyed hunting, especially falconry, and played chess and other board games with some zest and success. His reign came at a time of relative prosperity, when the medieval economy reached one of its peaks. It is generally accepted that the population of England reached well over four million by 1300, a figure it was not again to approach until the late fifteenth or early sixteenth century. The man and the resources were there to bring the English monarchy to a fine point of development.

The reign was certainly eventful, dramatically so in relation to British affairs, but not negligibly on the European stage. Edward's early years as king were spent consolidating his realm, repairing the ravages caused by the Barons' War. Faced by the Welsh problem in 1277 and again in 1282–3, he was decisive in his actions, and his military successes and political settlement of Wales rank among the greatest of his achievements. His later years were dominated politically by Scottish affairs, the 'Great Cause' of succession to the Scottish throne (1291–2) and his subsequent high-handed assertion of authority as Edward *malleus Scottorum*, Hammer of the Scots, which at times seemed near to success but resulted in ultimate failure. The situation was complicated by his war with France (1294–8) over Gascon problems, which sowed, in a way, the seeds of the Auld Alliance. Yet it is undeniable that under Edward I, England achieved an enviable success in the political and military fields, and gave for the greater part of the reign the true impression of a well-governed and prosperous community. The conquest of Wales, masterful actions in Scotland, regular summonses of parliament and a mass of positive Statute Law (1275–90) provide manifestations of the pride and strength of the English monarchy.

After 1294, and the outbreak of war with France, it is true that cracks appear in the smooth surface. Economic and fiscal troubles afflict the king and his advisers. Under pressure of financial need Edward was forced to confirm the charters in 1297 and to supplement them in 1300 with articles that, among other things, attempted to limit the use of the privy seal in matters touching the Common Law. The Scots proved impatient of the unnecessary harshness of English control and broke into sporadic rebellion. The last winter of Edward's life was spent in sickness at Lanercost priory, not far from Carlisle, and he died on 7 July 1307 at Burgh-by-Sands, not far from the Scottish border, a sick old man and yet still courageously leading his troops on campaign against the Scots. Anticipatory signs can be discovered of the impending troubles of the reign of his son, Edward II, in the constitutional as well as the political dimension. Yet for the most part the reign of this most formidable king can be read as a climactic point in the history of the English medieval monarchy. It is certainly a time by which the historian can truly reckon that England had been moulded into permanent shape.

At the top level in the constitutional field it is right to say that the king governed, but Edward accepted and encouraged the activity of the small royal council, which gained an increasing accuracy and clarity in definition as the reign proceeded. Councillors swore oaths to give good and loyal service and became more professional, drawn from the skilled lawyers and clerks of the household as well as from the baronial class. Their primary function was, indeed, to give counsel, and even Italian bankers and minor ecclesiastics attended councils to help with the king's business. The chancellor or the treasurer often presided in the king's absence, taking on heavy responsibility for the routine administrative work of the community, especially in financial matters. For much of Edward's reign the chancellor, Robert Burnell (1274–92), was the key man in government, heavily implicated in legal and financial affairs, and using the influential household office of the Wardrobe as the principal instrument of administration. Rumours over Burnell's personal greed, and doubts over his morals did not prevent Edward from giving him full support, and Burnell enjoyed the fruits of the see of Bath and Wells as its bishop from 1275 to the date of his death on 25 October 1292. The royal household preserved much of its undifferentiated nature, and it was only slowly – for example, under Burnell's successors – that the chancery itself began to acquire an independent official life. Walter Langton, the treasurer (1295–1307), bishop of Coventry and Lichfield, became the most important administrator in the later stages of Edward's reign, a man who had served his apprenticeship as a royal servant, first as clerk and then as keeper of the Wardrobe. Indeed, it was during his keepership (1290–5) that the organization of the Wardrobe reached its most complex and sophisticated form, as the key institution in the handling of royal administration. Custody of the privy seal rested in the Wardrobe, though it was clearly convenience at this stage, rather than any high theory, that determined whether or not a document should be issued in chancery under the great seal or by the Wardrobe under the privy seal. Relations with the Exchequer were also, as always, involved and tortuous, though to contemporaries they were probably simpler, more practical, and more dependent on the personalities of the great men and ministers around the king than we can always appreciate.

Active central administration was the preserve of the king, his household, the great officers, chancellors and treasurers, who were beginning to take on the aspect of permanent officers of state, and the compact small council. Two further developments of maximum importance to English institutional life reached a critical phase in the reign of Edward I: the formulation of regular assemblies known as parliaments, and the virtual creation of a legal profession associated with Common Law and the principal royal courts of law. The main principle behind the summons of great assemblies was simple – to establish the strongest links possible between royal government and the localities – and the king and his servants were fertile in experimenting to bring about that end. This was especially so in matters concerning finance. Clause 14 of Magna Carta laid down that scutage and all taxes apart from the customary aids were to be levied with the common counsel of the kingdom, and that the great barons were to be summoned to assemblies by individual writ. Gradually, the network of consent was widened, until in January 1265, under the pressure of civil war, de Montfort summoned knights of the shire and burgesses from the towns to such an assembly now commonly coming to be called a parliament. Edward extended and varied procedures, but held to the same basic principles. In 1295, in a famous example, he summoned to Westminster in the November the great prelates, bishops and abbots, lay barons, including 7 earls and 41 of the greater barons, 2 knights from each of the 37 shires, 2 burgesses from each of the 110 boroughs, and also representatives of the lower clergy. Their function was to consent to a tax that the king needed at that moment, an eleventh from the barons and knights, a seventh from the burgesses and a tenth from the clergy.

Many other assemblies, before and after 1295, were summoned with different compositions and varying functions – financial, legal and administrative; but one can quite see how it was that many later historians took the meeting of 1295 as a 'model' parliament. Some, though not all, of the essential elements in later medieval parliaments were present. Knights of the shire represented their own shire courts with full powers, and had the duty of reporting back the decisions of royal government to the shires; administration of the order to collect taxation at the agreed rate would be hard to implement without their active co-operation. In similar fashion, the select burgesses present at Westminster would act as key men in the collection of taxation on their return to their home boroughs. Parliament was not yet fully formed, however. The great feudatories, lay and ecclesiastical, met apart from the Commons, but this was no more than a foreshadowing of the later clear-cut division into two houses, Lords and Commons; the notion of a parliamentary peerage was not yet formulated. The presence of the lower clergy proved not to be a permanent feature. Parliament could not be said to limit the monarchy in any technical constitutional sense. It had still to win for itself a precise and permanent position in English government. Edward found it perfectly possible, though not very convenient, to rule for three years between 1302 and 1305 without parliament. Under his guidance, however, parliament in the sense of a properly constituted general assembly of the realm was well on the way to achieving a regular and recognizable role in the governance of the kingdom.

Legal as well as financial convenience prompted Edward's support for parliaments. The meetings provided suitable occasions for the presentation to the king of petitions, individual or corporate, asking that justice be done. This was a litigious age, and the growth of a legal profession, in the sense of both advocates and attorneys, is one of its most conspicuous features, helping to bind together in a more sophisticated manner the government of England in its legal attributes. A group of counsel, of sergeants (*servientes ad legem*) and their apprentices evolved under sanction from the king into professional pleaders at court, the ancestors of our present barristers. Attorneys (that is, men who will act as proctors for a principal) became more specialized, and in 1292 Edward made an attempt, through his justices, to ensure that a sufficient number of attorneys and apprentices should be appointed for every county; it was reckoned that 140 such men would be enough, that is to say 3 or 4 in each shire. The Common Law was so respected that it is no wonder Edward came to be regarded by later historians as the English Justinian. In fact, as Michael Prestwich has firmly demonstrated, the comparison is false. Justinian's fame rested on his codification of past law. Edward's successes rested on his reform of procedures, his speeding up of legal processes, and conspicuously in the shaping, between 1275 and 1290, of a great series of reforming statutes, an achievement which at face value gives an impression of *dirigisme*, in an almost modern sense, to Edward's activities.

A word needs to be said about these statutes, both in the positive sense and also with a note of caution. In nature and volume they represent a high point in the achievements of the English monarchy, giving a true and accurate picture of an active, creative central government at work. The litany of enactments is formidable: Westminster I (1275), the Statute of Jewry (1275), the Ragman Statute (soon after Michaelmas 1276), Gloucester (1278), Mortmain (1279), Acton Burnell (1283), Rhuddlan (1284), Wales (1284),

Westminster II (1285), Winchester (1285), Statute of Merchants (1285), *Quia Emptores* (1290), *Quo Warranto* (1290) – a tremendous achievement – with *de donis conditionalibus* (the first clause of Westminster II, which came to acquire statute status itself) and the later *de finibus levatis* (1299) indicating vital follow-through in critical areas concerning the transmission of land. The range is also impressive: land law, the relationship between lords and tenants, the problems of merchants facing the payment or non-payment of commercial debts, usury, the status of Jews (ultimately expelled in 1290), emendments to criminal law, with the general inclination to inflict more severe penalties in prison *forte et dure*. If all the statutes had been faithfully observed, England would have been as well-disciplined and equitable a society as was to be found anywhere in the Western world.

It is here that a note of caution has to be sounded. The statutes were the product of the reforming zeal of the king's council, anxious to learn from the dangers and disasters of the Barons' War of the 1260s and anxious to safeguard the future. Much of their content was the product of immediate troubles and, at times, personal plaints. Not until 1299 was the Statute Roll used to record statutes as issued; implementation depended on the courts and especially the judges. Blueprints for reform do not necessarily reveal the true state of affairs, and, in the matter of criminal law, for example, bitter complaints continued to be heard concerning the violence and unruliness of the community. To increase the severity of penalty for offences such as rape, assault or poaching was one thing; to secure convictions quite another.

Yet the judges were for the most part efficient, and the reign of Edward saw a steady flow of business away from private courts to royal courts, which could give judgments more speedily and enforce penalties more readily. Ralph Hengham was the greatest lawyer of the period, chief justice of the King's Bench from 1274 to his temporary disgrace in 1290, and then chief justice of Common Pleas from 1301. He was not free from the greed and speculation ascribed to many of his profession, and his disgrace and a very heavy fine came about as part of a regular purge of the judges undertaken by the king on his return from Gascony. Hengham was a cleric and a theorist as well as a practical lawyer, responsible for a tract, the *Summa Parva*, which discussed the implications of the detailed work embodied in Westminster II. By the end of the reign more and more of the key men in the legal world were drawn from specially trained students of law grouped into guilds or fraternities, which eventually in the fourteenth century developed into the Inns of Court, secular and professional in nature. It is no coincidence that reports on the most significant cases heard before the courts at Westminster began to be written down and published in the form of the Year Books from the 1280s until deep into the modern period. Lawyers and administrators were providing the political body of England with permanent and effective muscles and sinews.

Evidence of the will to confirm the unity of the kingdom of England is to be found from the earliest phase of Edward's rule, when he set in motion a massive inquest into royal rights and liberties, and into the activities of his own and other officers in the localities, sheriffs and bailiffs. The inquiry was quick and efficient. Pairs of commissioners were sent out into the shires, empowered to put some forty or so articles to local juries, asking what lands and rights had been lost to the crown and probing into corruption, extortion and inefficiency on the part of local officers. The whole job was done in a matter of four or five months between November 1274 and March 1275, and the results enshrined in a formidable set of Hundred Rolls. These provided Edwardian officers with information on which to base their reforming actions and, in their surviving form, present modern historians with their most powerful insight into the nature of medieval local government. The hundred remained a vital lesser unit in the political and military structure of the realm, whether in private or in royal hands (there were 270 hundreds in royal hands and 358 in private on Edward's accession), and the great royal inquiry helped to maintain the principle that all ultimately were responsible to the king. Even the most powerful lord held his hundred court as a franchise from the crown.

The strengthening and tightening of internal government represented in one respect no more than a means to an end: to achieve success in controlling the financial resources of the kingdom. Vast sums were raised successfully to pay for wars and major works.

41   Thirteenth-century map of Britain by Matthew Paris of St Albans.

45 An early fourteenth-century representation of the king deliberating in his parliament: from the *Modus tenendi parliamentum*.

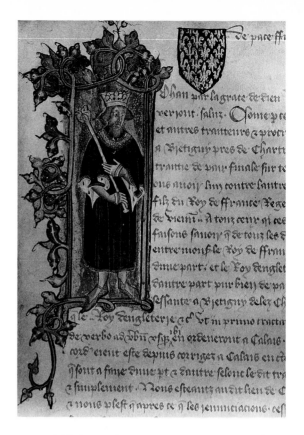

42 King John with his sceptre: from a thirteenth-century manuscript.

43 The charter of King John, providing for the annual election of a mayor of London: 9 May 1215.

44 The tomb of King John at Worcester cathedral.

Ir defer[...]
z Anglito[...]
[...]egis Et[...]
[...]iozes regi[...]
z Rege An[...]
probatus[...]
Regnum A[...]
[...]mm[...]
[...]van[...]

parliament[...] snmmoneri [...]

Archiepi Epi Abbes priozes

vt Baronum racone hninfmodi tenure

de qui pzo tennis sms repmatur vt sm

Etilis repntetur ad parliamentum illi

fnas de venendo z mozando ad parliamen[...]

ad parliamentum S set Rex solebat mfibz[...]

46 Aerial view of Old Sarum, bringing out the military strength of the site and also the size of the old cathedral.

47   Salisbury cathedral, which represents the full maturity of the early English Gothic style, built substantially c.1220–58. The tower and spire were added in the mid-fourteenth century.

49, 50 Aerial view and inner
face of the gatehouse of
Harlech castle, a dramatic
symbol of Edward's conquest
of Wales.

48 Westminster Abbey: the
choir looking east past the
high altar.

51   The best preserved of the Eleanor Crosses at Hardingstone, Northampton: the crosses were erected at every overnight stop of Eleanor's funeral cortège in 1290 from Harby to Westminster.

Vast armies of men were put in the field for civil and military purposes, and, on the whole, adequately paid. Constant concern over customs duties, notably the duty on the key export of English wool, and efficient management of the currency, culminating in a wholesale reminting (1299–1300), provide essential elements to the fiscal background of this intense human activity. Good records have survived of expenditure, and it has been estimated that Edward spent the huge sum of £80,000 or so on works in Wales alone between 1277 and 1304. At Chester and Flint in mid-August 1277, no fewer than 1845 diggers, 790 sawyers and 320 masons were employed. After the Welsh defeat in 1282–3 the castle-building policy was extended to Gwynedd. Some £9500 was spent over a $7\frac{1}{2}$-year period at Harlech, where, in the summer of 1286, 950 men were employed, though the establishment was reduced to a more or less care and maintenance number of 60 in the Welsh winter. Estimates for the building of Beaumaris in 1295 called for 2000 labourers, 400 masons, 200 quarrymen and 30 smiths. These men were drawn from all over England and Wales, and the resulting mobility, even if only of a temporary nature, should not be neglected as a contributing factor in the making of the English nation. Nothing binds people together as much as the feeling of sharing in a great enterprise. This was certainly true on the military side, and indeed came to apply not only immediately and to the English, but also, in the course of the Hundred Years' War, to the Welsh and English alike and conjointly.

We can say firmly that the idea of an English nation was fully formed by 1307 and that the extension of such an idea to Wales and to Scotland was much more than a pipe-dream. The dominant relationship of England and its king to Wales was confirmed, and a high proportion of the Welsh people, if turbulently, was successfully slotted in to English methods, English law and English enterprise. The Statute of Wales, issued at Rhuddlan, 19 March 1284, made provision for the shire system to be extended to the principality in the north, with the creation of Flint on the border and Caernarfon, Meirionydd and Anglesey in the heartland of the ancient kingdom of Gwynedd. Administrative arrangements were tightened in West Wales in the two shires of Carmarthen and Cardigan.

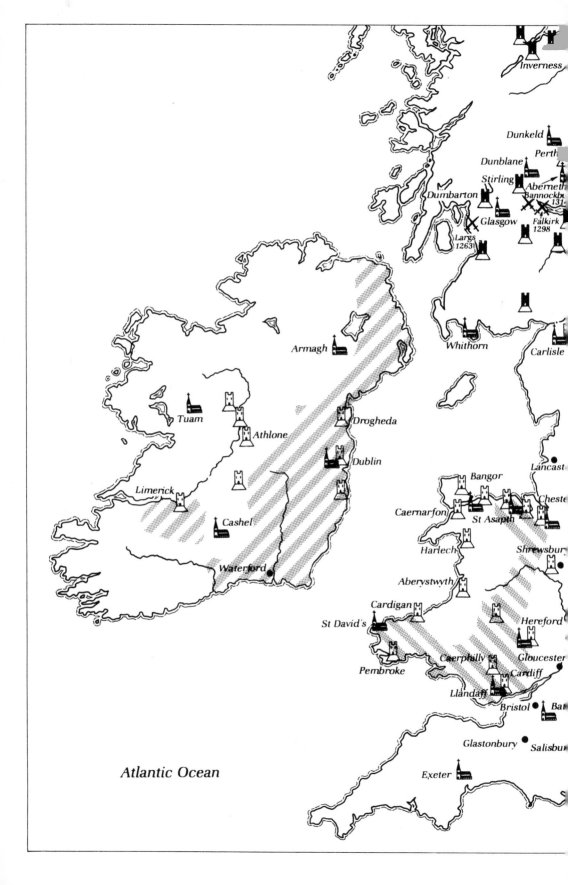

Inverness

Dunkeld

Perth

Dunblane

Stirling Aberneth

Dumbarton Bannockbu
                    131

Glasgow Falkirk
         1298

Largs
1263

Whithorn Carlisle

Armagh

Tuam Drogheda

Athlone Dublin

Lancast

Limerick Bangor

Cashel Caernarfon St Asaph Cheste

Waterford Harlech Shrewsbur

Aberystwyth

Cardigan Hereford

St David's

Caerphilly Gloucester

Pembroke Cardiff

Llandaff

Bristol Ba

Atlantic Ocean

Glastonbury Salisbur

Exeter

BRITAIN AND IRELAND IN THE LATE THIRTEENTH AND EARLY FOURTEENTH CENTURY

Cathedrals

Scottish burhs and castles

Some important castles

Irish dioceses to which English bishops were appointed in the 13th century

Welsh marcher lordships in the early 14th century

Hastings 1066 — Battles

0 20 40 60 80 100 Miles

Moray

Aberdeen

St Andrews

Edinburgh
Dunbar 1296
Berwick

North Sea

Newcastle
Durham

Richmond

Skipton
York

Pontefract
Conisborough

Grimsby

Lincoln

Sempringham
Boston

Leicester
Walsingham
King's Lynn

Peterborough
Worcester
Norwich

Northampton
Ely

Evesham 1265
Bedford
Bury St Edmunds

Cambridge

Ipswich

Oxford
Colchester

St Albans

London

Windsor
Canterbury

Winchester
Rochester

Southampton
Lewes 1264
Hastings 1066
Dover

Chichester
Wissant

Boulogne

FLANDERS

Antwerp

Ghent

Bouvines 1214

Lille
Tournai

Liège

Much Welsh law was preserved, but the new sheriffs and the principal officers, controllers, chamberlains and castellans were almost exclusively non-Welsh, English or Savoyard. Tax-collectors and recruiting agents were the immediate beneficiaries of the Welsh settlement and the shiring process, but so too were the adventurous young Welsh, if they were willing to take advantage of Edward's brave new world. At the battle of Falkirk in 1298, which swung the political balance in Scotland in Edward's favour, there were in the royal army 3000 cavalry, 14,800 English foot and 10,900 Welsh infantry still capable in practice of a degree of independent action. Edward did not altogether like or trust them. He is reputed to have grumbled at the height of the battle that both the Scots and the Welsh were his enemies; and indeed the Welsh held off their attack until it was quite clear that Edward was in the ascendant.

There still persist anomalies, and one must be careful not to make the whole process of unification appear too inevitable. With the benefit of hindsight it is easy to see that the critical institution that ensured success in the matter of nation-building was the shire court. The existence of the shire, given the state of communications and economic resources of the day, gave the king, his council and officers an ideal vehicle for the collection of taxes and supervision of local government. For all its diversity in local composition and in dialect, England was not too big to be governed. The strong element of local integrity in the shire and its institutions was an asset, centripetal not centrifugal. Baronial opposition, when aroused, tended to be personal and feudal, not comital. The king's writ ran almost universally, and the sheriffs and their underlings were empowered to see that the royal administration ran relatively smoothly. At the higher, more abstract level conscious efforts were made to foster the myth of the nation. Encouragement was given to the legends of Constantine, the Christian emperor born at York, as well as to Arthur and Glastonbury, the British descent from Troy and, more incongruously, Judas Maccabeus. To be king of England, inheritor of wealth and tradition, was a great achievement.

One still has to keep a sense of proportion and recognize the gulf that separated ideal from reality. King Edward was a French-speaking European; he lived linguistically in a Latinate environment. His baronial friends and knightly cronies spoke French; his devoted wife was Castilian. His son, and potential heir for the best part of a decade (October 1274–August 1284), was named Alphonse – a promising lad, to all account. Europe knew Edward as a powerful duke of Aquitaine who had performed homage to the French king for his lands held in France and who was prepared to spend much English treasure to defend his rights in Gascony; the Christian world recognized him as the leading crusader of his generation. In England itself the fissure between French-speaking lords and English subjects ran deep. Not until late in the fourteenth century could one be sure of the triumph of English as the language of England. The trauma of the Hundred Years' War and the genius of Langland, the poet of Pearl and Sir Gawayne, and above all Chaucer (*c.* 1340–1400) were needed to confirm that simple linguistic fact. Law, administration, effective government within finite bounds represented the reality of the state. In that sense, and it was a sense to endure, the England of Edward I was complete and permanent.

In the year of Edward I's coronation (1274) Thomas Aquinas, the greatest theologian of the Middle Ages, died at Fossanova, south of Rome, with his masterpiece, the *Summa Theologiae*, incomplete. In 1302, still touched by the euphoria of the jubilee celebrations of 1300, Pope Boniface VIII issued the papal Bull, *Unam Sanctam*, which stated an extreme case in favour of papal supremacy. Two years after Edward's death (1309) Dante was busy at his master political statement, ultimately embodied in his tract *De Monarchia*. Behind all three lay the shadow of Aristotle, guide and authority over so many tracts of human thought for much of the central Middle Ages. Man was by nature a political animal and the common thought of the age sought after a feeling for legitimate authority over a Christian people or peoples, including at best the principle of consent.

All three men, Aquinas, Boniface and Dante, powerful in their different fields of activity, looked for a unitary base to their concept of legal authority, hoping to see ultimately, if not immediately, a unitary expression given to it in political terms. To Aquinas, the least concerned with such problems, a vague notion of Christendom, to Boniface the papacy, and to Dante the Empire, provided institutional shape for such hopes: and yet the reality of Europe c. 1300 was very different. With hindsight we can see, in spite of the vehemence and rhetoric of the theorists, that whatever hankerings there had been for universal lordship in Western Europe were now things of the past. The Hohenstaufens had failed to create permanent control, and after the long interregnum (1254–73) the Empire emerged into the later Middle Ages with at most a superiority of prestige over other monarchies. The future in Germany and in Italy, and along the fault-line of Lorraine and Burgundy, lay with the princes and the great towns. Pope Boniface's assertion of supremacy was followed abruptly by his humiliation at Anagni (1303), his harsh treatment and subsequent death at the hands of the servants of King Philip IV of France.

For much of the fourteenth century the popes resided at Avignon subject to severe political pressure from the French kings. The political future lay with the more coherent national groupings of the West, finally to emerge as the kingdoms of Spain, France, and England. Basic notions of the just society and the rule of law applied equally to them as to the universal empires. Not without reason did Thomas Aquinas spend much intellectual effort on his concept of just war between states, whether Christian against Christian or Christian against pagan. In Spain the reign of Edward I's brother-in-law, Alphonso X, the Learned (1252–84), had witnessed the failure of universal schemes (he had hoped to become emperor) but the successful creation of a high sentiment of Castilian integrity in language, law and literature. In France, Philip IV (1285–1314: also brother-in-law to Edward after the English king's marriage to Margaret as his second wife in 1299) used the full weight of Roman law to build up a powerful autocratic monarchy, precociously centralized, ripe for the provincial disruptions of the Hundred Years' War.

England was more happily favoured in some important respects with her greater security as an island, longer traditions of local government, and more skilful articulation of central and local institutions. The fourteenth century was no happy period in the history of Western Europe with accounts of warfare and famine, plague and pestilence. Yet the nations had been substantially formed and it is from the political moulds of these Western monarchies – England, France, Spain, and to some measure Portugal – that the distinctive impress of the West was to make itself felt, as the world of the later Middle Ages and Renaissance opened up into the Age of Discoveries.

Select bibliography

Reliable general accounts are to be found in the relevant volumes of the *Oxford History of England*, notably Sir Frank Stenton, *Anglo-Saxon England* (3rd ed. 1971): replacement volumes for those produced in the original series are in preparation. For economic and social history basic interpretations are offered by H.R. Loyn, *Anglo-Saxon England and the Norman Conquest* (2nd ed. 1991) and E. Miller and John Hatcher, *Medieval England, Rural Society and Economic Change, 1086–1348* (1978). Good biographies of medieval kings appear in the series initially edited by D.C. Douglas: F. Barlow, *Edward the Confessor* (1970) and *William Rufus* (1983), D.C. Douglas, *William the Conqueror* (1964), W.L. Warren, *Henry II* (1973), and M. Prestwich, *Edward I* (1988). A mass of original material in translation together with splendid detailed bibliographical advice up to the date of publication is given in *English Historical Documents*, vol. I (to 1042), ed. D. Whitelock (2nd ed. 1979); vol. II (1042–1189), ed. D.C. Douglas and G.W. Greenaway (2nd ed. 1981); vol. III (1189–1327), ed. H. Rothwell (1975). D. Hill provides much valuable material in his *Atlas of Anglo-Saxon England* (1981).

Studies specially commended include:

C.J. Arnold, *Roman Britain to Saxon England* (1984)
S. Bassett, ed., *The origin of Anglo-Saxon kingdoms* (1989)
D. Bates, *Normandy before 1066* (1982)
    William I (1989)
P. Hunter Blair, *The World of Bede* (1970)
C.N.L. Brooke, *The Saxon and Norman Kings* (1963)
    (with Gillian Keir), *London 800–1216: the Shaping of a City* (1975)
R.A. Brown, *The Normans and the Norman Conquest* (2nd ed. 1985)
H.M. Cam, *The Hundred and the Hundred Roll* (1930)
J. Campbell, ed., *The Anglo-Saxons* (1982)
M. Chibnall, *Anglo-Norman England, 1066–1166* (1986)
S.B. Chrimes, *An Introduction to the Administrative History of Medieval England* (1952)
M.T. Clanchy, *From Memory to Written Record: England 1066–1307* (1979)
    England and its Rulers, 1066–1272 (1983)

R.H.C. Davis, *King Stephen, 1135–1154* (1967)
R.H.M. Dolley, ed., *Anglo-Saxon Coins* (1961)
J. Gillingham, *The Life and Times of Richard I* (1973)
J.C. Holt, *Magna Carta* (1965)
   Magna Carta and Medieval Government (1985)
   ed., *Domesday Studies* (1987)
S. Keynes and M. Lapidge, *Alfred the Great* (1983)
D. Knowles, *The Monastic Order in England* (2nd ed. 1963)
J. Le Patourel, *The Norman Empire* (1976)
W. Levison, *England and the Continent in the Eighth Century* (1946)
H.R. Loyn, *The Vikings in Britain* (1977)
   The Norman Conquest (3rd ed. 1982)
   The Governance of Anglo-Saxon England, 500–1087 (1984)
H. Mayr-Harting, *The Coming of Christianity to Anglo-Saxon England* (1972)
S.F.C. Milsom, *Historical Foundations of the Common Law* (1969)
J.N.L. Myres, *The English Settlements* (1986)
F.M. Powicke, *King Henry III and the Lord Edward* (1947)
S. Reynolds, *Kingdoms and Communities in Western Europe, 900–1300* (1984)
P.H. Sawyer, *The Age of the Vikings* (2nd ed. 1972)
   From Roman Britain to Norman England (1978)
A.P. Smyth, *Scandinavian York and Dublin* (2 vols: 1975 and 1979)
R.W. Southern, *St. Anselm and his Biographer* (1963)
   Robert Grosseteste (1988)
F.M. Stenton, *The First Century of English Feudalism* (2nd ed. 1961)
W.L. Warren, *King John* (2nd ed. 1978)
   The Governance of Norman and Angevin England, 1086–1272 (1987)
J.M. Wallace-Hadrill, *Early Germanic Kingship in England and on the Continent* (1971)
Ann Williams, ed., *Domesday Book: Studies* (1987)

Illustration acknowledgments

Bayeux: Centre Guillaume le Conquérant 24; The British Travel Association 11; Cambridge: Trinity College 29, 31 University Library 30; Peter Chèze-Brown 26, 36, 44, 49; F.H. Crossley 51; Dublin: Public Record Office 28; Durham: Cathedral Library 7, 8, 9; Florence: Biblioteca Laurenziana 10; Giraudon 25, 40; Martin Hürlimann 37; A.F. Kersting 48; Lichfield: Cathedral Library, Courtesy of the Dean and Chapter of Lichfield Cathedral 6; London: British Library 5, 21, 22, 23, 42, 45 British Museum 1, 2, 3, 4, 14, 15, 16, 18, 20, 38, 39, 41 Courtauld Institute of Art, University of London 32; National Monuments Record 33, 46; Public Record Office 27, 43; Royal Commission on Historical Monuments 50; New York: Pierpont Morgan Library 13; Oxford: Ashmolean Museum 17 Bodleian Library 12, 19, 35; Edwin Smith 34, 47

Index